# ·ESTHER·

*The Romance of Providence*

# ·ESTHER·

## The Romance of Providence

by

## J. VERNON McGEE

THOMAS NELSON PUBLISHERS
Nashville

Published in Nashville, Tennessee, by Thomas Nelson, Inc., Publishers and distributed in Canada by Lawson Falle, Ltd., Cambridge, Ontario.

Printed in the United States of America.

All Scripture quotations are from the King James Version of the Bible.

**Library of Congress Cataloging in Publication Data**

McGee, J. Vernon (John Vernon), 1904-
   Esther, the romance of providence.

   1. Bible. O.T. Esther—Criticism, interpretation,
etc. I. Title.
BS1375.2.M35    222'.906    81-22362
ISBN 0-8407-5796-4        AACR2

# ·CONTENTS·

# ·1·

## The Strange Providences of God

Providence is the hand of God in the glove of history.

*Providence* is a theological term. Dr. Strong, in his ponderous tome, defines it like this: "Providence is that continuous agency of God by which He makes all events of the physical and moral universe fulfill the original design with which He created it."

To explain it in layman's terms, there are three words that describe the work of God as it affects His physical universe.

1. There is *creation*, which explains the existence of the universe. By God's fiat He created all things. "In the beginning God created the heaven and the earth" (Gen. 1:1). We have only two alternatives today: We either accept revelation or we choose speculation. These are the only two explanations. And regardless of what you may believe, evolution is speculation. "Science" has no scientific explanation for the origin of the universe; it has to speculate. I accept revelation because it explains the origin of the universe without resorting to the speculations of men.

**2.** The second word is *preservation*, which explains the continuance of the universe. In other words, God not only created the cosmos, He holds it together. The Lord Jesus Christ is the Creator. He is also the Preserver. We are told in Hebrews 1:3, ". . . upholding all things by the word of his power. . . ." All things are held together by Him. Colossians 1:17 says, ". . . by him all things consist." Everything would come unglued today if it were not for Him. God Himself is holding together the atoms which are the building blocks of this universe.

**3.** The third word is *providence*, which explains the progress and development of the universe. Creation explains its origin, and preservation explains its continuance; but providence explains the progress and development of the universe. Providence is the means by which God directs all things—animate and inanimate, seen and unseen, good and evil—toward a worthy purpose, which means that *His will must ultimately prevail.*

The Word of God teaches this. For instance, Psalm 103:19 says, ". . . his kingdom ruleth over all." And notice Psalm 135:6: "Whatsoever the LORD pleased, that did he in heaven, and in earth, in the seas, and all deep places." God is running this universe to please Himself, not to please you or me. We are creatures; He is the Creator. We ought to get this straight in our thinking. The only freedom of speech that you and I have is that which *He* gives us. He is the Creator. We are creatures.

Also notice verses 7–10 of Psalm 135:

He causeth the vapours to ascend from the ends of the earth; he maketh lightnings for the rain; he bringeth the

wind out of his treasuries. Who smote the firstborn of
Egypt, both of man and beast. Who sent tokens and
wonders into the midst of thee, O Egypt, upon Pharaoh, and upon all his servants. Who smote great nations, and slew mighty kings.

God takes the responsibility for doing those things.
In Daniel 4:35 it is written:

And all the inhabitants of the earth are reputed as
nothing: and he doeth according to his will in the army
of heaven, and among the inhabitants of the earth: and
none can stay his hand, or say unto him, What doest
thou?

In other words, God does not have to report to anyone
concerning His conduct. God runs this universe and
He runs it His own way. That is what providence
means. Paul, in Ephesians 1:11, expresses it thus, ". . .
who worketh all things after the counsel of his own
will."

You may think that is too theological, so let me put it
like this: Providence is God at the steering wheel of
this universe. It is the way God coaches the man who
is on second base. Providence means that God is behind the scenes, shifting and directing the happenings
of the world. Or, as we have had it expressed, God
stands in the shadows, keeping watch over His own.
Or, again, providence is the hand of God in the glove
of history, and that glove will never move until He
moves it.

The Book of Esther teaches the providence of God.
Actually, the name of God is not mentioned in the
Book of Esther, and for this reason there were those
who did not want it included in the canon of Scripture.
However, the Book of Esther is a revelation of the

people of God out of the will of God. They are walking in a willful pathway; no appeal is made to Him by name in the entire Book of Esther. But God will over-rule their attitude, and He will protect them.

The word *providence* means "to provide." God will provide. Providence means that God is back of His creation today, back of the human race, back of those who are His own by redemption. And God is giving men and women direction in the world today.

In the Book of Esther we see that this is how God works. The young Jewish girl Esther was chosen by King Ahasuerus to be queen of Persia. She was not queen for a day; she was queen for a lifetime. Furthermore, she was chosen by means of a beauty contest. Many people simply would call her lucky. But God was behind these events. Her cousin Mordecai happened to overhear a plot to slay the king. Yes, he was "lucky" to have overheard it. But God was over-ruling. Mordecai reported the plot, but his loyalty went unrewarded. The king didn't recognize him at all. (Say was that unlucky!) Then to make matters worse, Mordecai incurred the wrath of Haman (whom the king had promoted to a very influential office) by refusing to bow to him. In revenge, Haman deter-mined to destroy not only Mordecai but all his people throughout the kingdom.

Then one night the king could not sleep. Since no sleeping pill was available, he called for the book of records of the kingdom, the chronicles—what we would call the "minutes" of the kingdom. Believe me, minutes are boring, I don't care whose they are. And these minutes were boring, too. They had a few excit-ing items in them, like accounts of occasional murders, but when nothing else would put the king to sleep, those minutes would do the trick. Yet on this night he was alerted because the servant read the particular page that recorded what Mordecai had done to save the king's life. The king asked the question, "Was he rewarded?" "No," the servant said, "he wasn't rewarded." And the king said, "Well, we are going to reward him." King Ahasuerus made that decision at exactly the right psychological moment. The entire sequence of events sounds like luck—it was luck on the human plane—but God was directing. And God saved an entire people from extermination because of it.

Now providence is not confined to the Book of Esther. You will find it running as a bright thread all the way through the Word of God.

Joseph is an example (see Gen. 37–45). This man Joseph, without doubt, was the champion hard luck boy. At seventeen years of age, this young fellow, the favorite of his father, was given a coat of many colors. He had a wonderful advantage at home, but his brothers plotted against him. They wanted to murder him. Worse than that, they sold him into slavery, and he was carried down into the land of Egypt. For a seventeen-year-old boy, that was terrible. However, he recognized the hand of God in his life and he began to advance, for he had been sold to an Egyptian official. Just as he got to the top, the rug was pulled out from under him, and he found himself thrown into prison. We would expect him to give up, but he didn't. He interpreted dreams for Pharaoh's baker and butler, who were also in prison. When the butler was released, Joseph said to him, "Now, be sure to tell Pharaoh about me, because I'm down here and I'm not guilty. I would like to get out." But the butler forgot all about him, and Joseph spent at least a couple of years more in prison. In two years you can become very discouraged in prison when you are not guilty! This boy—I marvel at him—seems to have ridden on top of the waves all the time. The hand of God was in his life. God by His providence was directing him. One day Pharaoh had a dream and the butler said, "I remember my sins today—I forgot all about that boy. I know somebody who can interpret your dreams." Actually, it would have been the worst thing in the world if the butler had told Pharaoh about Joseph two years earlier. Joseph would have gone back home, and he would not have been available to interpret the dreams of Pharaoh. God kept Joseph in prison, for God was preserving His people. Later on, Joseph could look back on his life and say, even to the brothers who sold him as a slave, ". . . ye thought evil against me; but God meant it unto good . . ." (Gen. 50:20).

God has put in your life enemies, and He has done so for your good. Oh, we cry and we go to the wailing wall, complaining and whining, but God permits trying situations in our lives for a purpose.

David Harum had some very old-fashioned wisdom to dish out years ago. He said that God permits a dog to have a reasonable amount of fleas and it is a good thing, for it enables the dog to take his mind off the fact that he is a dog!

God permits an enemy or trouble to come into our lives so we will turn to Him. The only way He can get the attention of a great many folk is by sending them trouble! Perhaps you have had that experience: You turned to God when trouble came to you, but you would not have come otherwise. God permits this to happen.

Shakespeare put it like this: "There is a divinity which shapes our ends, rough-hew them how we will." Someone else has suggested that disappointment should be spelled with a capital "H"—"His appointment." God permits disappointments, enemies, and even tragedies to come to us. He does so for a purpose.

Another book in the Bible, Ruth, has the romance of redemption for its theme, but it also illustrates the providential dealings of God. One morning Ruth went out from the town of Bethlehem to find a field in which to glean. She knew nothing of the surrounding countryside. I walked down that road purposely during my travels to Israel, and I looked on every side. I'll be honest with you, I wouldn't have known which field to choose. It was very important which field Ruth chose, because if she had not gone into the right field, the prophecy that Micah gave (5:2) would have been wrong—Christ would not have been born in Bethlehem. (Send word to the wise men not to come; they will not find Jesus in Bethlehem!) But Ruth did go into the right field, and we are told, ". . . her hap was to light on a part of the field belonging unto Boaz" (Ruth 2:3). From her standpoint it was chance, but God by His providence was directing.

The writer of the Proverbs made this very arresting statement:

The lot is cast into the lap, but the whole disposing thereof is of the LORD (Prov. 16:33).

God is saying that you cannot even go to Las Vegas and throw the dice but what He is there seeing how they come up. "The lot is cast into the lap." And the Greeks had a saying like this, "The dice of the gods are loaded!" God says to you and me, "Don't gamble with Me—I'll win. *I* know how it is coming up. You don't." So many people gamble with their lives at stake today. My friend, you don't gamble with God.

Ruth looked to God. I know she prayed. Yet God never revealed His will to her. He guided her by His providence, as He will guide any willing soul today.

One of the most interesting cases of God's providential dealings concerns old Ahab, king of Israel. He was a man far from God. First Kings 22 records the alliance between Ahab and Jehoshaphat (which Jehoshaphat should never have made) to go to war against Syria. Ahab pulled a good one. He went into battle in the uniform of a common soldier so that only Jehoshaphat could be identified as a king—and Jehoshaphat almost got killed because the Syrians took out after him. They were looking for the top man, the king of Israel, and Jehoshaphat was dressed as royalty. Ahab was chuckling, "They won't get me. I'm well protected by my disguise." When they took out after Jehoshaphat, Ahab probably wiped his brow and said, "I made it." But in the Syrian army there "happened" to be a trigger-happy soldier. We are told, "And a certain man drew a bow at a venture, and smote the king of Israel between the joints of the harness [armor]: wherefore he said unto the driver of his chariot, Turn thine hand, and carry me out of the host; for I am wounded" (1 Kin. 22:34).

Ahab was fatally wounded. You see, that arrow had

Ahab's name on it. That soldier put an arrow in his bow, pulled it back, and let it go. He wasn't aiming at anything.

A little boy got a B B gun for Christmas. After the boy had tried it out, a friend asked him, "What did you hit?" He said, "Nothin'." "Well," asked the friend, "what did you shoot at?" "Nothin'," said the little boy.

My friend, this soldier aimed at nothing, but he hit Ahab. And the king was killed because God had said through Micaiah the prophet that this would happen (see 1 Kin. 22:13–17).

By the providence of God, Caesar Augustus signed a tax bill. If you had leaned over his shoulder and said, "That's interesting! This bill will cause a prophecy given by Micah over seven hundred years ago to be fulfilled," he would have laughed and said, "I know nothing about that. I need taxes. I have a huge army to maintain, and I need to carry on the poverty program here in Rome." So he signed the tax bill that moved Mary and Joseph to Bethlehem in fulfillment of Micah 5:2.

The psalmist wrote long ago, "For the kingdom is the LORD's; and he is the governor among the nations" (Ps. 22:28). Yes, God was and is in control.

One day a young man was arrested. His name was Stephen; the verdict was handed in; and they stoned him to death. We are told that in the midst of all the trouble,

He [Stephen], being full of the Holy Ghost, looked up stedfastly into heaven, and saw the glory of God, and Jesus standing on the right hand of God, and said, Behold, I see the heavens opened, and the Son of man

standing on the right hand of God. Then they cried out
with a loud voice, and stopped their ears, and ran upon
him with one accord, and cast him out of the city, and
stoned him: and the witnesses laid down their clothes
at a young man's feet, whose name was Saul (Acts
7:55–58).

When that young man looked up and said, "I see
the heavens opened and the Son of man standing on
the right hand of God," the crowd all cried out, "This
is blasphemy." And Saul of Tarsus, a brilliant young
Pharisee and the biggest skeptic of all, led the group.
They put their coats at his feet, and he directed the
stoning of Stephen. After he looked down at the
bloody body of that boy lying there, he looked into the
heavens, realizing that Stephen had something he did
not have. And a few days later, on the way to Damascus, Saul spiritually was prepared for what happened
(see Acts 9). There was a blinding light, and the Lord
Jesus Christ Himself spoke to him. God by His providential dealings used Stephen's testimony to prepare
Saul for the appearance of Jesus on the Damascus
Road.

The examples of God's providence are not confined
to the Bible. They are evident in secular history. All
you have to do is open your eyes.

God stopped Xerxes. God had said through Daniel
(see Dan. 8) that He was going to move the center of
world power out of the East, from Asia and Africa, to
Europe. He did so when Xerxes lost the Battle of Thermopylae. How could Xerxes lose? The Greeks were
masters on the ocean; yet they could not match the
three hundred vessels of Xerxes. But God could. In my
travels in Greece we stopped by the Bay of Salamis,

and I took several pictures of the site of the battle. As I looked out over Thermopylae, a modern port today, I thought of the storm that destroyed three hundred of Xerxes' vessels. A single storm shifted the power from the East to the West and changed the entire destiny of the world. God moves in the affairs of men.

Napoleon said that God is on the side of the biggest battalions, but he was wrong. He had the biggest battalions at Waterloo, and he lost.

The Spanish Armada was anchored off the coast of England. The next day England would have gone down in defeat, but that night a storm came. When the morning broke, the Spanish Armada was wrecked, and Great Britain became the proud leader of the seas for three hundred years. The destiny of the world was changed.

The hand of God has been in our own nation. You cannot read our history without recognizing the fact that God has moved in the history of this nation. When Columbus was coming to the Western Hemisphere the first time, he was headed directly to either the coast of Virginia or the Carolinas. A flight of pigeons went by and he followed them. Consequently, the Spanish flag went up on South America and the West Indies, while Protestantism came to this country. South America has more natural resources than North America has ever had, yet it has lagged and the story is told in religion. May I say to you, God was directing the affairs of this nation.

During the Revolutionary War, Benedict Arnold betrayed his country. He gave the entire blueprint of West Point to Major André of the British forces. Major André was riding on horseback toward the British lines with those blueprints in his boot. He came to a crossroad and did not know which road to take—but God knew. Down the road he chose were Revolutionary soldiers. If he had not made the big mistake of saying the wrong thing, they never would have searched him. But he spoke, and they searched him, and they discovered the awful betrayal and saved our country.

In the early days of America the colonists stayed too close to the eastern seaboard. They were afraid to penetrate the vast expanse of the Middle West. Eventually God waved a little gold, and the Gold Rush was underway. A lot of people came to California. They didn't all find gold, but they've been coming ever since. That was one way God moved.

You may be saying, "Yes, God guides nations—I can see that—but what about people today? What about the individual who has turned his or her back on God? Is there any hope?"

Certainly there is. That is the kind of people I am interested in. In the forty-second chapter of Isaiah, verse 16, there is an arresting statement. After presenting "my servant" (the Lord Jesus Christ) and talking about the nation Israel, God says:

> And I will bring the blind by a way that they knew not; I will lead them in paths that they have not known: I will make darkness light before them, and crooked things straight. These things will I do unto them, and not forsake them.

God says the person who does not know, who cannot see the way, or who has ruled Him out is still under His care. God will lead such a person by a way that he or she knows not.

May I use a personal example? The first time I preached in Los Angeles was a Sunday evening. I had come to California as a tourist. Apparently, very few people knew that a "famous" preacher from a little town in Texas was preaching, because not many folk were in attendance that evening. However there was a lady in the congregation—a very distinguished looking lady—who, when an invitation to accept Christ was given, raised her hand. The one who talked with her after the service related her story to me. This woman had come to California from the Chicago area in search of one of her children. A daughter, movie crazy and hoping to crash into stardom, had headed for Hollywood, and the mother had lost contact with her. Of course the woman was frantic. She had been unsuccessful in her search, and finally had gone to the railroad station to return home. With five hours to wait for her train, terribly disturbed in her own mind and heart, she began to walk. She heard chimes playing and finally located the source, the church where I was preaching. Years later, the counselor told me that she had received letters from the woman, telling how those few hours had been the turning point in her life. She had come into the church that night in a suicidal frame of mind, for she thought everything had gone black for her. Accepting Christ was the greatest moment in her life.

Do you know how she found that church? By the providence of God.

A doctor was attending a medical convention in a downtown hotel. From what he told me, it had been a pretty rough Saturday night. He was far from God. He got up in the morning, looked out his window, and saw the sign, "Jesus Saves." And he came to the church where I was preaching that morning. He said later, when he told me about the experience, "I knew the message was for me from the beginning. When you gave the invitation, not a hand went up and I knew for sure that you preached this one for me. I went back to my room and got down on my knees." "Thru the Bible" is on the radio station in Yakima, Washington, today because of that doctor. Do you know why he came to church? Because of the providence of God.

I would quit preaching if it were not for the providence of God. His providence is what makes life thrilling and exciting. Neither you nor I know what is around the corner, but God by His providence is leading.

Look at the plight of this "now" generation. The philosophy being taught in a majority of our colleges today is one of the aimlessness of life, the purposelessness of life, and the meaninglessness of life. Yet God by His providence had an aim, a purpose, a meaning for you in mind millions of years ago. Today He wants to direct you. Why don't you let Him?

Every day is a new adventure for a child of God. He brings into our lives enemies and trouble, but He also brings sweetness and love, blessings, light and abundant life. He alone is the One who can do that today, and He wants to do it for you.

Abraham took his son Isaac to the top of Mt. Moriah (which today lies within the walls of Jerusalem). He built the altar, he arranged the wood, the fire was ready, and his son said, "Dad, here is the altar, the wood, and the fire, but where is the lamb?" Listen to Abraham: ". . . God will provide himself a lamb . . ."

(Gen. 22:8). "God will provide . . . ." *Provide* is my word; *providence* means "to provide." "God will provide Himself a Lamb."

Now do not be confused about the ram that got caught in a bush. That was a *ram*, not a lamb. Abraham and Isaac looked around and there was no lamb; there was a ram caught in the thicket. Nineteen hundred years later a Man walked into that area where Abraham had offered Isaac and of Him John the Baptist said, ". . . Behold the Lamb of God, which taketh away the sin of the world" (John 1:29).

God has provided a Lamb of sacrifice for you, friend. I do not know what the specific needs of your life are today, but I know this: You need the Lamb of God to take away your sin. You need Jesus. He can save you and He can make your life meaningful and purposeful.

The oil fields of east Texas were probably the last rough and tumble oil fields that this country had. In that area was a dirt farmer, a man who was uneducated but very shrewd. Oil was discovered on his land, and he was sharp enough not to sell. He became an independent oil operator and grew immensely wealthy. He built a magnificent home. He had a lovely wife and two little boys. This man was as godless, as wicked, as vile and profane as any person who has walked this earth.

Then a flu epidemic hit east Texas. His wife and one of the little boys died.

Two friends who were pastors in that area told me the story. One of them pastored a church nearby and went to visit the man that evening. The pastor was ushered into this lovely, spacious home. There were the two caskets, and there sat the man. The pastor went over to sit beside the man and started to put his arm around him to comfort him. The man shrugged him off and began to curse him. "I had never heard language like that," the pastor told me. "He cursed me as I had never been cursed before, and he cursed God. 'What right had God to take my wife and my little boy?' he said."

A few short years went by. Then early one morning, as I was waiting to air my program at the radio station in Dallas, the news commentator who preceded me announced that an explosion had occurred at the New London school in east Texas. Five hundred children and teachers were killed, I learned later. It was one of the greatest tragedies this country has ever had.

The oil man knew his little boy was at the school. He rushed to the scene of the explosion and, not seeing his child anywhere, began to dig like a madman in the debris and rubble. Finally, someone called to him. His son had been found—dead. The father gathered the little boy into his arms and paced up and down the school yard as if he were insane. Finally, the man was taken home, and the little body was placed in a casket.

My pastor friend knew he had to go through the ordeal again. He drove to the mansion, knocked on the door, and was ushered in. Over against the wall was one small casket, and there sat the father huddled over, crushed and broken. The pastor steeled himself for what he was sure would come. Not daring to put his arm around the man or even to touch him, he simply said, "I have come to comfort you the best I can." The man looked up, tears coursing down his cheeks, and said, "I have known all along that God was after me, but I didn't know He would have to do this to get me." That man came to Christ.

The providence of God can be tender, as it was with Abraham, or it can be severe, as it was with the oil executive and with Joseph. By His providence God moves in lives today, and He wants to move in your life, freely. Let us take a good, long look at how God moved in the lives of those who lived in a godless land—as seen in the account of Esther—and see what lessons there are for us, living in our world today.

# ·2·

## The Wife Who Refused
## To Obey Her Husband

*Esther, Chapter 1*

Now it came to pass in the days of Ahasuerus,
(this is Ahasuerus which reigned, from India even
unto Ethiopia, over an hundred and seven and
twenty provinces:) that in those days, when the
king Ahasuerus sat on the throne of his kingdom,
which was in Shushan the palace, in the third year
of his reign, he made a feast unto all his princes
and his servants; the power of Persia and Media,
the nobles and princes of the provinces, being
before him: when he shewed the riches of his
glorious kingdom and the honour of his excellent
majesty many days, even an hundred and fourscore days. And when these days were expired,
the king made a feast unto all the people that were
present in Shushan the palace, both unto great
and small, seven days, in the court of the garden
of the king's palace; where were white, green, and
blue, hangings, fastened with cords of fine linen
and purple to silver rings and pillars of marble: the

beds were of gold and silver, upon a pavement of red, and blue, and white, and black, marble. And they gave them drink in vessels of gold (the vessels being diverse one from another,) and royal wine in abundance, according to the state of the king. And the drinking was according to the law; none did compel: for so the king had appointed to all the officers of his house, that they should do according to every man's pleasure. Also Vashti the queen made a feast for the women in the royal house which belonged to king Ahasuerus.

On the seventh day, when the heart of the king was merry with wine, he commanded Mehuman, Biztha, Harbona, Bigtha, and Abagtha, Zethar, and Carcas, the seven chamberlains that served in the presence of Ahasuerus the king, to bring Vashti the queen before the king with the crown royal, to shew the people and the princes her beauty: for she was fair to look on. But the queen Vashti refused to come at the king's commandment by his chamberlains: therefore was the king very wroth, and his anger burned in him.

Then the king said to the wise men, which knew the times, (for so was the king's manner toward all that knew law and judgment: and the next unto him was Carshena, Shethar, Admatha, Tarshish, Meres, Marsena, and Memucan, the seven princes of Persia and Media, which saw the king's face, and which sat the first in the kingdom;) What shall we do unto the queen Vashti according to law because she hath not performed the commandment of the king Ahasuerus by the chamberlains? And Memucan answered before

the king and the princes, Vashti the queen hath
not done wrong to the king only, but also to all the
princes, and to all the people that are in all the
provinces of the king Ahasuerus. For this deed of
the queen shall come abroad unto all women, so
that they shall despise their husbands in their
eyes, when it shall be reported, The king Ahasuerus commanded Vashti the queen to be brought
in before him, but she came not. Likewise shall
the ladies of Persia and Media say this day unto all
the king's princes, which have heard of the deed
of the queen. Thus shall there arise too much
contempt and wrath. If it please the king, let there
go a royal commandment from him, and let it be
written among the laws of the Persians and the
Medes, that it be not altered, that Vashti come no
more before king Ahasuerus; and let the king give
her royal estate unto another that is better than
she. And when the king's decree which he shall
make be published throughout all his empire, (for
it is great,) all the wives shall give to their husbands honour, both to great and small. And the
saying pleased the king and the princes; and the
king did according to the word of Memucan: for
he sent letters into all the king's provinces, into
every province according to the writing thereof,
and to every people after their language, that every man should bear rule in his own house, and
that it should be published according to the language of every people.

This chapter out of the history of a pagan nation is
inserted in the Word of God for a very definite pur-

pose: to teach the providence of God, as we shall see as we turn the pages of this book.

The story begins with the law of a heathen kingdom and a difficulty—a matrimonial difficulty. It was a very personal affair that arose in this kingdom, but it had international repercussions.

In order to relieve any anxiety that might be in the hearts of some, I digress to say that if you wish to know how Christians ought to get along in marriage, you should read the fifth chapter of the Epistle to the Ephesians. In fact, you should read the entire epistle. When you come to the passage that reads, "Wives, submit yourselves unto your own husbands, as unto the Lord" (Eph. 5:22), you must continue to read, because Paul adds, "Husbands, love your wives, even as Christ also loved the church, and gave himself for it" (Eph. 5:25). Women, if you are married to a godless husband, God never asks you to be obedient to him. In speaking of the married life of Spirit-filled believers, God does say that if you are married to a man who is willing to die for you because of his love for you, then you ought to be submissive to that man. Where there is perfect love there should be perfect happiness in submission. Certainly that is the Christian ideal, for it is used by God to illustrate the relationship between Christ and His church. However, the events of the Book of Esther took place in a pagan culture, where God's instructions were not considered.

The first thing we shall attempt to do is to identify Ahasuerus. As previously suggested, this king is probably the Xerxes of secular history. Understand that *Ahasuerus* was not the name of the man but his title. The word means "high father" or "ruler." As the word

*Caesar* is a title and does not identify the man, so *Ahasuerus* does not identify this Persian king in secular history. Archaeological discoveries have confirmed the belief of many scholars that *Darius* (which means "maintainer"), *Ahasuerus* (which means "venerable king," "high father," or "a king worthy of reverence") and *Artaxerxes* ("great king"—"great" as to character, rule, and empire) were titles, and may have referred to the same person at different periods of his life as his greatness increased.

There is quite a divergence of opinion concerning the identity of the Ahasuerus of the Book of Esther. The viewpoint that I hold is that he was Xerxes the Great of Persia, because that man was the one who actually brought the Medo-Persian Empire to its zenith. Xerxes was the man who made the last great effort of the East to overcome the West, and it was a tremendous effort. Evidently the banquet referred to in the Book of Esther was the one in which he brought together the leaders of his entire kingdom, to sell them, if you please, on the idea of making a great campaign against Greece. From the time the forces of Xerxes came to Thermopylae until Japan's attack on Pearl Harbor in the twentieth century, no Eastern power had made a bid for world domination. Xerxes—Ahasuerus—was a man of tremendous ability and probably one of the greatest of the world rulers.

The banquet recounted in the Book of Esther causes anything that humans might attempt in these days to pale into insignificance. We are told that ". . . in the third year of his reign, he made a feast unto all his princes and his servants. . ." (1:3). We have already been told that there were 127 provinces, and out of each of these he brought a delegation (how many, I don't know), so that he had present probably one thousand or two thousand people for this banquet! You can see that it was no little private supper that he was having.

The record continues, "When he shewed the riches of his glorious kingdom and the honour of his excellent majesty many days, even an hundred and fourscore days" (1:4). For 180 days he boarded these fellows! He had a perpetual smorgasbord for six months! The father of Louis XV of France is said to have talked with the preceptor and the exchequer of his kingdom about this banquet, and he said that he did not see how the king had the patience to have that kind of a banquet. The exchequer, who was handling the finances for Louis XV, said that he did not see how he financed it. When you have just a few friends in for Christmas dinner, you know what it costs you for turkey and all the trimmings. It's an expensive sort of an affair. Well, you can imagine the expense that this man incurred. He brought the feast to a climax in the last seven days: "And when these days were expired, the king made a feast unto all the people that were present in Shushan the palace, both unto great and small, seven days, in the court of the garden of the king's palace" (1:5). Apparently Ahasuerus brought in a tremendous population of people for the final seven days in the court of the garden.

The description of Shushan in verse 6 has always interested expositors of the Word. There are those who find in it all kinds of spiritual meaning. I must confess that I have to agree with Dr. Ironside and other men who, when they get into this maze, can find

no spiritual meaning whatsoever. You will notice that
the colors are a little different from what we are accus-
tomed to seeing in the Bible as pertaining to God's
people. The colors in the tabernacle were largely red
and blue and purple. There was white, of course, and
gold and silver. But here you find two other colors
introduced, green and black, that did not appear in
any word that God gave concerning the tabernacle or
concerning the New Jerusalem.

This banquet revealed the wealth, the luxury, and
the regal character of this Oriental court. The reason
for it is obvious. Ahasuerus had called in all of his
princes and all of his rulers from every corner of his
kingdom that he might win their wholehearted support for the military campaign to capture Greece. He
intended to make himself the supreme ruler of the
world. And, of course, Ahasuerus almost succeeded in
that attempt. I am confident he would have succeeded
had God not already determined that the operation
would end in failure and that the center of world
dominance would be shifted from the East to the West.

We have seen Ahasuerus' method of strategy used
on a comparably small scale in our day. Several years
ago, when one of the great automobile concerns came
out with a new model, they brought all of their dealers
from all over the world to Detroit for a convention. The
convention was made up of drinking parties and banquets, with the idea of selling the dealers on the new
model before it came out.

So it was with Ahasuerus, only he was bidding for
support of a new model campaign. He was going to
attempt something never before done by the East:
domination of the West.

Ahasuerus' banquet, a pagan event from the beginning, ended in a drunken orgy. However, we are told that "the drinking was according to law; none did compel" (1:8). Even these pagan Oriental rulers who had absolute sovereignty never forced anyone to drink, although they themselves were given to it. Today we are more "civilized": A person either has to drink or get out!

One evening a lumberman in Tacoma, Washington, came into a hotel lobby where I was sitting, waiting for someone to pick me up for a meeting. The man sat down with me and began to talk, and I discovered that he was a fine Christian. I asked, "Aren't you going to the banquet they are having here?" He said, "Yes, but this is the cocktail hour, and I never attend it." I asked, "How do you get by, not attending it?" And he said, "I just happen to own the lumber company." Then he added, "But I'll have to go in there in thirty minutes and listen to some of the silliest conversation that you've ever heard! When you are sober, you don't like to listen to it." There was a man of high caliber who had to put up with that sort of thing.

Back in the days of the Persian kingdom the law was that a man did not have to put up with it—"none did compel."

"Also Vashti the queen made a feast for the women in the royal house which belonged to king Ahasuerus" (1:9). She made a feast for the women's auxiliary. The men who had come had brought their wives, but women couldn't go to the main banquet—which makes it different from some present-day banquets, by the way. Women were kept in separate quarters, so Vashti held a separate banquet for them.

"On the seventh day, when the heart of the king was merry with wine" (1:10) means, in the language of the street, the king was "high" on the seventh day. The question arises concerning not only this king but any king or ruler: Is he a fit ruler if he is engaged in drunkenness? It is said that the Oriental people today are asking if America with all of her drunkenness is in a position to be the leader of the nations of the world. This is a question that America must answer within the next few years. Drunkenness, and not the neutron bomb, could be the thing that would take us under. If drunkenness continues as it is today, it will ultimately destroy our land.

Under the influence of alcohol, Ahasuerus did something that he would never have done if he had been sober. He commanded the chamberlains who served in his presence to bring Vashti to the banquet. He had displayed his wealth and his luxury, and he had demonstrated to the princes and rulers his ability to carry on the campaign he had in mind. Under the influence of alcohol, he attempted to make a display that was contrary to the proprieties of that day. He tried to display Vashti, who was a beautiful woman to look at. Ahasuerus decided that he would bring her into the banquet court before that convention of men. He would never have done so had he not been drunk.

This queen (she is going to be put aside—moved off the stage, so to speak—and we will not see her again) was a noble woman of a pagan culture. She refused to go. "But the queen Vashti refused to come at the king's commandment by his chamberlains. . ." (1:12). Believe me, that revealed a scandal in the kingdom: The king was having trouble with his queen! She refused to come, and I admire her for her decision.

Perhaps you thought I was going to say that she made a grave mistake. I will come to that conclusion in a minute, but let me first say that Vashti was absolutely right, or justified, in not coming; she did not have to come. According to the etiquette of that day, she did not belong in such a gathering of men, so this queen refused her king's commandment. She stood instead under the protection of her rights, and I admire her for that. There was no law at that time that would compel her to come; therefore she stood and said that she would not.

You can imagine the king getting up at the banquet and announcing, "Now, gentlemen, I have a real treat for you. I have sent for my queen. I want you to see her. She's a beauty. I want to introduce her to you so that you can see all the wealth and the wonder of this kingdom." And then in a few moments a chamberlain walks up behind him and whispers, "She won't come." Imagine having to get up and say, "I'm very sorry, gentlemen, but we've had to change the program of the evening. Our main attraction didn't arrive; we'll not be having the queen this evening."

Well, that started the buzzing throughout the banquet. The thousand or more guests probably began to say, "Is he a king, or is he not a king? What kind of king cannot even command his queen?" Although Vashti was perfectly justified in refusing to come, I think she should have thought the situation over in this manner: *I can refuse and I probably ought to refuse. But this is a scandal that will get out and this will hurt my king, my husband. I think, under the circumstances, I'll go.* On that basis, she should have gone to the banquet. She should have obeyed.

There is a spiritual application for us here. The body

of believers, the church, is called the bride of Christ. And the church's task in this age is to display her beauty to the world. But are we fulfilling our responsibility? We the church are wrapped up in our own little programs. We are not too concerned about the lost, are we? Do you know there is a world outside that is going to hell? How much do we really care? The church has been called upon to obey our husband, Jesus Christ.

There is a lovely picture presented in the Song of Solomon of a husband and his bride. This is the bride speaking:

> I sleep, but my heart waketh: it is the voice of my beloved that knocketh, saying, Open to me, my sister, my love, my dove, my undefiled: for my head is filled with dew, and my locks with drops of the night (Song 5:2).

The husband, the bridegroom, has been out witnessing, looking for lost sheep, and he wants her to join him in this. He is a picture of Christ.

But where is the bride, the church? She says,

> I have put off my coat; how shall I put it on? I have washed my feet; how shall I defile them? (Song 5:3).

The home has a dirt floor, and the bride says, "I'm in bed; I am comfortable; I have already washed my feet. I don't intend to get up and soil them again." That is the position of the church in our day. We have come to the place of comfort; we do not want to go out after the lost.

> My beloved put in his hand by the hole [latch] of the door, and my bowels were moved for him. I rose up to open to my beloved; and my hands dropped with myrrh, and my fingers with sweet smelling myrrh, upon the handles of the lock (Song 5:4,5).

It was a lovely custom of that day that when the bridegroom came to the house and could not get in, he would reach inside and put myrrh on the handle of the door. This was like sending a bottle of perfume to the bride. Finally when the bride in the Song came to open the door for him, she found there only the myrrh, the sweet fragrance of his presence.

It is wonderful today to study the Word of God; it is good to have our groups for fellowship, but outside our comfortable lives is a world that has not heard the gospel. Let me ask you this question: What are you doing now to get the gospel out to this lost world? Honestly, what are you doing? Lots of folks in our churches are busy as termites, but the activity is all on the inside of the church. They are not obeying their King who said, ". . . Go ye into all the world, and preach the gospel to every creature" (Mark 16:15). The Lord Jesus has said that we are the light of the world. His command is, "Let your light so shine before men, that they may see your good works, and glorify your Father which is in heaven" (Matt. 5:16). The church today is like Queen Vashti, saying that she will not go.

This brings to mind the tremendous story told by Dr. J. Wilbur Chapman many years ago. It illustrates the great love of our Shepherd, the One whom we should represent today. He told of one of the great sheep dogs in the Swiss Alps. One cold night when heavy snow was falling, the shepherd brought in the sheep but three of them were missing. He looked down at this great dog, warmly bedded down with her little puppies for the night, and said to her, "Go get the three sheep." This intelligent dog looked up, then put her head down again, for she did not want to go. The shepherd gave the command again. Then this great shepherd dog got up, left her puppies, and went out into the snow. She was gone for several hours. When she returned with two of the sheep, she was torn and bloody. She settled herself with her puppies. The shepherd looked at her and said, "There is still one missing. Go, get the sheep." And the dog again got up and went out into the dark, stormy night. After a period of several hours the dog returned; this time she could hardly walk, but she had the last sheep. What a picture this is of our Savior. What a picture it should be of His church!

Let us look again at Queen Vashti and her refusal to do the king's bidding. It called for a crisis meeting of the cabinet. The king's advisors talked over this new development, for it was no incidental matter. They were preparing for a great campaign, and suddenly the queen would not obey the command of the king. What should be done with her?

One member of this cabinet was a henpecked husband by the name of Memucan. How do I know he is henpecked? Look at this fellow! "And Memucan answered before the king and the princes, Vashti the queen hath not done wrong to the king only, but also to all the princes, and to all the people that are in all the provinces of the king Ahasuerus. For this deed of the queen shall come abroad unto all women, so that they shall despise their husbands in their eyes, when it shall be reported, The king Ahasuerus commanded Vashti the queen to be brought in before him, but she came not" (1:16,17). In other words, he was saying, "Something must be done about this, because I don't dare go home!"

Perhaps you have heard of the henpecked husband

who came to the office one morning and boasted, "Last night my wife was down on her knees before me." One of the fellows, knowing the situation, was a little skeptical. He said, "What were the circumstances, and what exactly did she say to you?" The husband looked a little embarrassed and admitted, "Well, she was down on her knees, looking under the bed, and she said, 'Come out from under there, you coward!'"

That's Memucan. He was a henpecked Mr. Milquetoast. He was saying, "Something must be done to protect our homes in this matter." Actually this was a real crisis, because the king and the queen set an example for the kingdom. Notice Memucan's proposal. "If it please the king, let there go a royal commandment from him, and let it be written among the laws of the Persians and the Medes, that it be not altered, That Vashti come no more before king Ahasuerus; and let the king give her royal estate unto another that is better than she" (1:19). Memucan's recommendation was radical surgery: "Let's eliminate this woman who refuses to obey."

You may be thinking, "Doesn't the Bible teach that a wife is to obey her husband?" No, it does not. You cannot find that in the Word of God. Obedience was imposed upon wives in Oriental and other pagan cultures, but this never has been true among Christians. You may challenge that statement because in the fifth chapter of Ephesians Paul says, "Wives, submit yourselves unto your own husbands, as unto the Lord" (Eph. 5:22). But let's look at what that command really means.

To begin with, Paul speaks here of the Spirit-filled

life. He commands us to be filled with the Spirit and mentions the things that will result from being filled with the Spirit. And I do not think there can be a right husband-wife relationship without a filling of the Spirit on the part of both. Actually I don't believe you can even sing to God unless you are filled with the Spirit of God; I don't believe you can preach a sermon or teach a Sunday school class unless you are filled with the Spirit of God. And I do not think you can have a right husband-wife relationship unless you are filled with the Spirit of God.

When Paul says, "Wives, submit," he is not saying to obey, but to respond to your husband. God has made man and woman in such a way that the wife is a responder and the husband a leader. The husband always takes the lead—or at least he should. All God is saying to the woman is, "Respond to your husband." When the man says to the woman, "I love you," she is to respond by saying, "I love you." But suppose the husband doesn't love; suppose the husband does not say, "I love you." Then God does not ask her to say that she loves him. Suppose the husband is brutal. The wife will respond in kind. Anytime a man comes to me and says, "My wife is cold," he gives himself away. She is responding to the kind of husband he is. God never asks any woman to obey a godless man. You cannot find that in the Word of God. "Wives, submit yourselves unto your own husbands" speaks of a Spirit-filled relationship; God says to the wife, "Respond to your husband," and to the husband, "Love your [wife], even as Christ also loved the church, and gave himself for it" (Eph. 5:25).

Understanding these truths only throws the setting

for the Book of Esther—a pagan court—into sharper relief. The pagan law enacted had nothing to do with the Mosaic Law and was not Christian by any means. Ahasuerus and his council made a new law, but it was the law of the Medes and the Persians: ". . . That Vashti come no more before king Ahasuerus; and let the king give her royal estate unto another that is better than she.

"And when the king's decree which he shall make shall be published throughout all his empire, (for it is great,) all the wives shall give to their husbands honour, both to great and small. And the saying pleased the king and the princes; and the king did according to the word of Memucan: For he sent letters into all the king's provinces, into every province according to the writing thereof, and to every people after their language, that every man should bear rule in his own house, and that it should be published according to the language of every people" (1:19–22).

The law concerning Vashti reveals to us today the character of Ahasuerus, who I believe was Xerxes in secular history. You will recall that he took his army, the largest that ever had been marshalled, as far as Thermopylae, and led a fleet of three hundred ships, which were destroyed at Salamis. After that defeat, in a fit of madness Xerxes went down to the sea and beat the waves with a belt for destroying his fleet. Now a man who would do that evidently has something radically wrong with him. Apparently he was a man who suffered from some form of abnormality, as many rulers have—and still do. Julius Caesar, Napoleon, Hitler were men of abnormal mental processes. Nebuchadnezzar, great man that he was, represented in Daniel (see 2:38) by the head of gold, suffered from an abnormality known as hysteria (see Dan. 4:33). Any man today who even wants to be a world ruler ought to be examined by a psychiatrist! However, forms of abnormality have not kept men from achieving greatness in the history of the world. And this was true of Ahasuerus. He was a man of tremendous ability. Yet in unreasoning anger he allowed this banishment of his lovely queen. It became the law of the Medes and the Persians, an edict which could not be altered. Although later the king himself wanted to break the law, he could not. The law of the Medes and the Persians could not be broken.

Here was a man's law that could not be changed or altered in any way whatsoever, nor could it be revoked. Even the king himself had to bow to this law. Then what about the laws of God? God has laws whether you like them or not. He has said, "The soul that sinneth, it shall die . . ." (Ezek. 18:20). That law cannot be changed. The "new morality" and our changing culture cannot alter it. Sin is still sin, and God says, "The soul that sinneth, it shall die." The law has not been changed today. God will not change it. God cannot Himself change it. Do you know why? Because He would be untrue to His own nature. He would deny His own attributes and His own character. Of course He would never do that. "The soul that sinneth, it shall die" stands at this moment. "Well," someone says, "that leaves the human race in a terrible plight because God also says, 'All have sinned, and come short of the glory of God' " (Rom. 3:23). That's correct. But, you see, these laws of God have been superseded by a higher law, the law of a Savior who came down to this earth to die upon a cross. Jesus

Himself gave His reason for coming to this earth: ". . . the Son of man came not to be ministered unto, but to minister, and to give his life a ransom for many" (Mark 10:45). God, without changing His law one iota, sent His Son to take your place and my place. Since He could not change His law, "The soul that sinneth it shall die," Jesus Christ was made sin for us and He died in our stead.

The Lord Jesus also said, "I came not to call the righteous, but sinners to repentance" (Luke 5:32). Why? There is none righteous to call. But He has come for *sinners*. Those are the only ones He saves. You see, we must be willing to accept God's estimate of us: We are sinners. Dr. Hudson Taylor made that statement to a man one day, and the man objected, "I don't feel like a sinner." Dr. Taylor said, "If you don't feel like one, then believe God: You are." God says we are sinners. Take God's word for it.

In San Francisco during World War II, I saw a ship at the dock that was loaded and ready to sail. One of the officers told me, "We have to wait for the tide to come in. That ship is so loaded that nothing in the world can lift it but the tide." When the tide came in, the ship went out. I crossed the Atlantic on the *Queen Mary* once. We boarded her about seven o'clock in the evening, but the announcement was made that we would not sail until morning. The ship had been delayed coming in because of a storm in the Atlantic, and she could not go out because the tide was out. But when the tide came in, the water lifted that great ship. At four o'clock in the morning we felt our vessel moving out to sea. The law of the tide overcame the law of gravity.

It is still true that "The wages of sin is death" (Rom.

6:23). It is still true that "The soul that sinneth, it shall die." But, thank God, there is another law in operation. There is a Savior who, because of His vicarious death, can reach down and in His marvelous grace receive you and take you home to glory.

# · 3 ·

## *The First Beauty Contest To Choose a Queen*

*Esther, Chapter 2*

After these things, when the wrath of King Ahasuerus was appeased, he remembered Vashti, and what she had done, and what was decreed against her. Then said the king's servants that ministered unto him, Let there be fair young virgins sought for the king: and let the king appoint officers in all the provinces of his kingdom, that they may gather together all the fair young virgins unto Shushan the palace, to the house of the women, unto the custody of Hege the king's chamberlain, keeper of the women; and let their things for purification be given them: And let the maiden which pleaseth the king be queen instead of Vashti. And the thing pleased the king; and he did so.

Now in Shushan the palace there was a certain Jew, whose name was Mordecai, the son of Jair, the son of Shimei, the son of Kish, a Benjamite; who had been carried away from Jerusalem with the captivity which had been carried away with Jeconiah king of Judah, whom Nebuchadnezzar the king of Babylon had carried away. And he brought up Hadassah, that is, Esther, his uncle's daughter: for she had neither father nor mother, and the maid was fair and beautiful; whom Mordecai, when her father and mother were dead, took for his own daughter.

So it came to pass, when the king's commandment and his decree was heard, and when many maidens were gathered together unto Shushan the palace, to the custody of Hegai, that Esther was brought also unto the king's house, to the custody of Hegai, keeper of the women. And the maiden pleased him, and she obtained kindness of him; and he speedily gave her her things for purification, with such things as belonged to her, and seven maidens, which were meet to be given her, out of the king's house: and he preferred her and her maids unto the best place of the house of the women. Esther had not shewed her people nor her kindred: for Mordecai had charged her that she should not shew it. And Mordecai walked every day before the court of the women's house, to know how Esther did, and what should become of her.

Now when every maid's turn was come to go in to king Ahasuerus, after that she had been twelve months, according to the manner for the women, (for so were the days of their purifications accomplished, to wit, six months with oil of myrrh, and six months with sweet odours, and with other things for the purifying of the women;) then thus came every maiden unto the king; whatsoever she desired was given her to go with her out of the house of the women unto the king's house. In the evening she went, and on the morrow she returned into the second house of the women, to the custody of Shaashgaz, the king's chamberlain, which kept the concubines: she came in unto the king no more, except the king delighted in her, and that she were called by name.

Now when the turn of Esther, the daughter of Abihail the uncle of Mordecai, who had taken her for his daughter, was come to go in unto the king, she required nothing but what Hegai the king's chamberlain, the keeper of the women, appointed. And Esther obtained favour in the sight of all them that looked upon her. So Esther was taken unto king Ahasuerus into his house royal in the tenth month, which is the month Tebeth, in the seventh year of his reign. And the king loved Esther above all the women, and she obtained grace and favour in his sight more than all the virgins; so that he set the royal crown upon her head, and made her queen instead of Vashti. Then the king made a great feast unto all his princes and his servants, even Esther's feast; and he made a release to the provinces, and gave gifts, according to the state of the king. And when the virgins were gathered together the second time, then Mordecai sat in the king's gate. Esther had not yet shewed her kindred nor her people; as Mordecai had charged her: for Esther did the commandment of Mordecai, like as when she was brought up with him.

In those days, while Mordecai sat in the king's gate, two of the king's chamberlains, Bigthan and Teresh, of those which kept the door, were wroth, and sought to lay hand on the king Ahasuerus. And the thing was known to Mordecai, who told it unto Esther the queen; and Esther certified the king thereof in Mordecai's name. And when inquisition was made of the matter, it was found out; therefore they were both hanged on a tree: and it was written in the book of the chronicles before the king.

The second chapter of the Book of Esther opens with the phrase "after these things." After Ahasuerus returned to his palace without Vashti, he recognized how lonely he was. The record tells us, ". . . he remembered Vashti, and what she had done, and what was decreed against her" (2:1). According to the law of the Medes and the Persians, Ahasuerus himself, though he was the supreme ruler, was not able to change his own law—although by this time I am sure he wanted to do so. Vashti had been set aside forever. The law of the Medes and the Persians could not be altered.

Those who were around the king—his cabinet, those who were ruling with him or who occupied high positions—noticed how moody he was and how lonely, and they made a suggestion. The suggestion was, very candidly, that there be conducted a beauty contest the like of which Atlantic City and Long Beach never have seen or heard. The entire kingdom was searched for beautiful women, and they were brought in from that wide kingdom, near and far. You can well imagine the number that were brought in—I'm sure it was in the hundreds. The king was to be the judge, the sole judge, of this contest.

Esther's story begins with verse 5 of chapter 2. "Now in Shushan the palace there was a certain Jew, whose name was Mordecai, the son of Jair, the son of Shimei, the son of Kish, a Benjamite [of the tribe of Benjamin]." The question that immediately arises is: What is *he* doing here? God had permitted His people to return to their own land, as He had prophesied (see 2 Chr. 36:22,23). Cyrus was to give a decree to permit them to return, and those who were in the will of God did return to Palestine. However, very few returned to their homeland—less than sixty thousand. The greater number of them had made a place for themselves in the land of their captivity. They had learned shop-keeping from the Gentiles and had elected to remain.

Have you ever noticed that the Jew, when he is in Palestine, is a farmer, but when he is out of Palestine, he's a shopkeeper (or anything but a farmer)? This is true today. When I was in Palestine, guides pointed this out with delight: Here was a man who had been a brilliant scientist in Germany, who was now living in a kibbutz and working with his hands out in the field. I was amazed to see how the Jews have gone back to the soil in Palestine. But the Jews of Esther's day had learned shopkeeping from the Gentiles in Babylon and they liked it. When they were free to go, they did not want to return to Jerusalem. Many of them, out of the will of God, chose to remain in a pagan culture, and Mordecai happened to be one of them.

Mordecai should have been back in his homeland, but notice where he was of all places: in the palace of

Persia. He had a political job. You may remember that
Joseph also had a political job in Egypt, yet he was in
the will of God directly; Daniel in the court of Babylon
was in the will of God; but Mordecai was not in the
direct will of God. You will see that Esther is the book
of the providence of God. As I have said, if you want a
popular definition of providence: Providence is how
God coaches the man on second base. And this man
Mordecai was brought to home base, although he was
out of the will of God and although he was not looking
to God for help. Even at a time when you think he and
his people would have turned to God, they did not.
There is no mention of God or of prayer in this book at
all, because these people were out of the will of God.

Both Mordecai and Esther come on the page of
Scripture in a poor light, although they prove to be
very noble individuals, as we shall see later in the
story. Mordecai had been taken captive, probably at a
young age, in Nebuchadnezzar's second deportation
of captives from Jerusalem. That was during the reign
of Jeconiah (better known as Jehoiachin). The first
deportation that had left Jerusalem was made up of the
princes, the nobility, and the upper class. Daniel was
with that group. The second captivity had taken those,
shall we say, of the upper middle class. And this man
Mordecai was in that group. After the third deportation, when Jerusalem was finally destroyed, only the
poorest class was left in the land.

Mordecai had a young cousin, whose parents may
have been slain in Nebuchadnezzar's taking the city,
for multitudes were slain. Her Hebrew name was
Hadassah, and he adopted her as his own daughter. If
you go back to Palestine today, you will see one of the

finest hospitals in the world. A great deal of research is being done there. It is the Hadassah Hospital, named for this young Hebrew woman.

Notice what is said concerning her. "And he brought up Hadassah, that is, Esther, his uncle's daughter: for she had neither father nor mother, and the maid was fair and beautiful; whom Mordecai, when her father and mother were dead, took for his own daughter" (2:7). She had one asset (and it is an asset), and that was beauty. Beauty is God's handiwork, and it is wonderful to see that it can be dedicated to Him. I wish today that the devil did not get so much that is beautiful in this world, but he does. If God has blessed you with good looks, offer that to Him for He can use it.

When the announcement was made that there was to be a choice of another queen for Ahasuerus, immediately Mordecai was interested. He took his young cousin Esther and entered her in the beauty contest. "So it came to pass, when the king's commandment and his decree was heard, and when many maidens were gathered together unto Shushan the palace, to the custody of Hegai, that Esther was brought also unto the king's house, to the custody of Hegai, keeper of the women" (2:8). You see the providence of God moving into this situation. "And the maiden pleased him [that's no accident], and she obtained kindness of him; and he speedily gave her her things for purification, with such things as belonged to her . . ."(2:9).

An interesting fact comes to light in verse 10: "Esther had not shewed her people nor her kindred: for Mordecai had charged her that she should not shew it." Remember that Mordecai and Esther were a part of a captive people, and anti-Semitism always has been a curse in the nations of the world. And it had been in Babylon. You cannot read the account of Nebuchadnezzar's destruction of Jerusalem without realizing his hatred for these people. He was the first to bring them to Babylon, but by Esther's time a new nation—Persia—was in charge. Yet the anti-Semitic feeling remained, and Mordecai, being very sensitive to that, warned Esther not to reveal her nationality. That silence was tantamount to a denial of her religion, and religion is the very thing that had identified God's chosen people down through the years. The moment Mordecai and Esther denied their nationality, that moment they denied their religion.

You remember that Jonah did the same thing on board ship. He had revealed neither his nationality nor the fact that he believed in and worshipped the living and true God. In going to Tarshish he was out of the will of God. Mordecai and Esther, by remaining in the land of captivity, were out of the will of God. Because of this they had no witness for God. It is of interest to note that today, when men and women are out of the will of God, they have very little to say about their faith in Christ.

Mordecai is not resting upon God at all. He doesn't turn to Him in prayer, and we read, "Mordecai walked every day before the court of the women's house, to know how Esther did, and what should become of her" (2:11). This man, out of God's will, paces up and down, nervously biting his fingernails, wondering how the contest will come out. He has not, nor can he, put his worries into God's hands. I'm not sure that he knows anything about the providence of God. But

God is overruling in this. May I remind you of our definition of providence? Providence is the way that God leads the man who will not be led. We see Him beginning to move at this particular point in the story of Esther. It is no accident that Esther is given the most prominent place, or that she is shown every favor and is given every consideration. There are no accidents with God.

Notice the type of beautification (called "purification") that went on. "Now when every maid's turn was come to go in to king Ahasuerus, after that she had been twelve months, according to the manner of the women, (for so were the days of their purifications accomplished, to wit, six months with oil of myrrh, and six months with sweet odours, and with other things for the purifying of the women)" (2:12). May I say to you, men, that if your wife takes a few hours in the beauty salon, you ought not to complain. These girls spent a whole year there! The first six months they went to the spa for reducing and for oil treatments. Then the next six months they went to the perfumers. I suppose they even swam in cologne in order to be prepared to go into the presence of the king. You can see the tremendous emphasis that was placed on physical beauty, and this is typical of pagan cultures. The farther away America gets from God, the more counters we have in our department stores for beauty aids. Have you noticed that? (And with the multiplicity of beautifying treatments, it is rather disappointing that we don't have more beauty than we do today.) But these girls went through an entire year of beauty conditioning for the contest.

Notice the awful chance that Esther takes. "In the

evening she went, and on the morrow she returned
into the second house of the women, to the custody of
Shaashgaz, the king's chamberlain, which kept the
concubines . . ." (2:14). If she does not win, she becomes a concubine of the king of Persia, which certainly would have been a horrible thing for this Jewish
maiden. That is the reason Mordecai is biting his fingernails. Out of the will of God, he knows the awful
chance this girl is taking.

Yet, God is going to overrule. Notice: "Now when
the turn of Esther, the daughter of Abihail the uncle of
Mordecai, who had taken her for his daughter, was
come to go in unto the king, she required nothing but
what Hegai the king's chamberlain, the keeper of the
women, appointed . . ." (2:15). When her time comes
she requires no more than is appointed for a contes-
tant to wear. She goes in her natural beauty and stands
before the king. ". . . And Esther obtained favour in
the sight of all them that looked upon her" (2:15). God,
you see, is overruling. Esther has not yet let anyone
know her background and her race.

"So Esther was taken unto King Ahasuerus into his
house royal in the tenth month, which is the month
Tebeth, in the seventh year of his reign. And the king
loved Esther above all the women, and she obtained
grace and favour in his sight more than all the virgins;
so that he set the royal crown upon her head, and
made her queen instead of Vashti" (2:16,17). He does
not have to look any further; the contest is over as far
as he is concerned. He has found the one to take
Vashti's place, and Esther is made queen.

We are told that the king loved Esther. I must confess that I am not impressed by that statement at all.

Those of you who have read my book on Ruth know
the emphasis put upon the romance of Boaz and Ruth,
the loveliest love story, I think, that has ever been told.
It is a picture of Christ's love for His church. But I have
to say that I do not find that quality here. This was an
old, disappointed king who almost had reached the
end of the road. I am reminded of the story of a
foreigner who came to this country. He asked, "What
are these 'three R's' that I keep hearing about in this
country?" Some wiseacre gave him this answer: "At
twenty it's romance; at thirty it's rent; and at fifty it's
rheumatism." Well, it was rheumatism with this man
here. Ahasuerus was an old king, and Esther was a
lovely young girl. He was an old pagan with no knowl-
edge at all of what real love in God might mean to a
couple. I must say that I cannot see anything in the
text to wax eloquent about or to say, as some have
done, that this is a picture of Christ and His church. I
do not see that at all.

However, the event was of utmost significance. It is
thrilling to hear how this girl, belonging to a captive
people, suddenly became queen over one of the
greatest gentile empires the world has ever seen. The
wave of anti-Semitism that was imminent would have
blotted out these people, and God's entire purpose
with Israel would have been frustrated. But when the
wave hit, Esther was in a unique position. How did
she get there? By the providence of God. *God* moved
her into that place.

Esther was not in God's direct will. The Mosaic Law
was clear: Neither she nor any one of her people were
to marry a Gentile. But Esther had stooped in order to
conquer. In this lies another great lesson for God's

children. There are many things in this world that
God's people do, and in the doing are out of His will.
In spite of it all, God will overrule and make circumstances work out for His glory and the fulfillment of
His purpose. I have in mind a very clear example of
this. Repeatedly people ask me the question: Do you
believe that women preachers are scriptural? No, I do
not believe that women preachers are scriptural. There
are many passages in the Bible to support my statement. The next question usually is: How then do you
explain the fact that many women preachers have
been and are being wonderfully blessed by God? May I
say to you that in spite of the fact that women
preachers are not God's direct will, God will always
bless His Word when it is given out. There are many
things today that are not in accordance with God's
will, but He overrules them for His glory. Esther was
disobeying God absolutely, but that did not mean that
she was out from under the control and care of
almighty God.

You will remember that this book opened with a
feast. Now Ahasuerus held another feast: Esther's
feast. "Then the king made a great feast unto all his
princes and his servants, even Esther's feast; and he
made a release to the provinces, and gave gifts,
according to the state of the king" (2:18). With a lovely
queen to take Vashti's place, Ahasuerus was so jubi-
lant he suspended taxes for one year. If such a decree
were made in our day, it would rock the world! But it
is interesting to see that the king did have that authority to suspend taxes for a year.

"And when the virgins were gathered together the
second time, then Mordecai sat in the king's gate"

(2:19). "Sitting in the king's gate" means that Mordecai had a new position—not a job, a position. It means he was a judge, for the courthouse of the ancient world was the gate of the city. Most of the cities were walled, and sooner or later all the citizens would pass through the gate. Court convened at the city gate, not at the courthouse in the town square. The city gate was the place Boaz went to have a legal matter taken care of. Lot sat in the gate, which meant that he had gotten into politics in Sodom and had a judgeship.

Isn't it interesting that when Esther became queen, the next thing you know Mordecai was a judge, sitting in the gate? That was nepotism—getting your kinfolk into office. I do not know whether Mordecai was made judge because of his ability or because Esther whispered in the ear of the king, "This man Mordecai has been just like a father to me. He is a man of remarkable ability, and I think you ought to give him a good position." The king may have said, "Well, that's interesting. We've just had an opening for a judge here at the east gate, and I'll give him that position." Esther is a very human book, you see, and politics haven't changed a bit, have they?

"Esther had not yet shewed her kindred nor her people; as Mordecai had charged her: for Esther did the commandment of Mordecai, like as when she was brought up with him" (2:20).

Esther was a rather remarkable person. Even married to the king, she took instructions from the man who reared her! And probably Mordecai is one of the outstanding men in Scripture to whom we have paid very little attention. Apparently he was a man of remarkable ability.

At this point in the story something takes place that seems extraneous; yet it is upon this incident that the whole book hinges. As someone has said, "God swings big doors on little hinges." Again we see the providence of God; He was moving behind the scene. "In those days, while Mordecai sat in the king's gate, two of the king's chamberlains, Bigthan and Teresh, of those which kept the door, were wroth, and sought to lay hand on the king Ahasuerus" (2:21). This is a very familiar scenario: an Oriental potentate, and fellows with long mustachios, hiding behind pillars, plotting against the king. Actually, intrigue in an Oriental court was common; there seemed always to be someone who was after the king's job. Mordecai's new position gained him a vantage point so that he was able to overhear the plot. "And the thing was known to Mordecai, who told it unto Esther, the queen; and Esther certified the king thereof in Mordecai's name" (2:22).

I suppose that Esther said to the king, "You remember that I recommended Mordecai as a judge, and you can see that he is already doing a very excellent job. He has discovered a plot against your life!" The "FBI" investigated and found it to be true. "And when inquisition was made of the matter, it was found out; therefore they were both hanged on a tree. . . ." There wasn't even a trial. All Ahasuerus had to do was give the word. And the incident ". . . was written in the book of the chronicles before the king" (2:23).

It is interesting to see that Mordecai was not rewarded for what he had done. That omission is important. I suppose he brooded over it many times, wondering why in the world he had been ignored. God is overruling. Chapter 2 of Esther in a very special way reveals the theme of the book: the providence of God.

There is abroad in our midst today the notion that if circumstances are not favorable, God is not in them. A young student once came to me for counseling. He said that he felt that perhaps he was out of the will of God. When I inquired why he felt so, he replied that circumstances were growing difficult for him, and his subjects in school were becoming harder than he had anticipated. In short, he was finding so many obstacles that he felt he was not in accord with the purposes of God for his life. I find that many folk reach this decision through just such reasoning. However, circumstances are no indication at all, for God was moving in Esther's affairs, and He was moving in the affairs of Mordecai.

God is moving today by providence. I love the story of Vaughn Shoemaker, the Christian cartoonist. God in His providence chose this boy. He was a poor boy, but he had a wonderful mother of prayer. He grew up with an older brother who felt that prayer and religion generally were for sissies. Instead of finishing his education, Vaughn took odd jobs, and in the course of time he met a young woman with whom he fell in love. When he proposed to her, she startled him by saying that she would not let him ruin her life, as well as his own, by not having a definite occupation and purpose in life. If he would prove that he wanted to establish himself under the guidance of God, then she, as a Christian girl, would be interested.

He went to his older brother and asked for the necessary financial assistance to enter the Chicago Art Institute. The loan was made, but the Art Institute dismissed him, saying they did not think he would ever become a cartoonist. Shortly afterwards he was able to secure a position with the *Chicago Daily News*. Then came the "break"—some call it luck, but he calls it providence. The head cartoonist was given a position in New York City; the second in charge went to Features; the third had to leave because of illness in his family, and Vaughn was the only one left in the office. The editor called him in and said, "Vaughn, draw something until I can get another cartoonist." The editor never did secure another cartoonist, for Vaughn Shoemaker proved his abilities and soon his drawings went into syndication.

Vaughn tells the story of how he was called to the hospital where his elder brother was desperately ill. Realizing that this brother who had helped him so much could not live much longer, he asked, "Roger, do you know Christ as your Savior?" Roger smiled and said, "Yes, I do," and he was gone. Vaughn left that place of parting, went to his own room, and upon his knees gave his life to God. From that moment he has never drawn a cartoon without first kneeling to ask God to direct him. His cartoons reveal deep insight and imagination and often carry a Christian message of intrinsic value. God has led that man through the years. Long before he knew Him, God was leading, bringing him to Himself.

Finally, let me tell the story of a man who began listening to our radio program in the San Francisco Bay area. He was a contractor and a Roman Catholic. I was teaching the Book of Romans at the time, and he has since told me, "If I could have gotten to you, I would have punched you in the nose for the things you were saying." God, in His providence, tuned him in; he would get angry and tune out. "But the next morning," he said, "I always was right there waiting for you." In the providence of God, the man was transferred from the San Francisco Bay area to Los Angeles, where he is now. For about three months, he came to the church that I was pastoring on Thursday night for Bible Study, going down the street to confession beforehand. Finally one night, after three months, he gave his heart to the Lord. How did it happen? By God's providence.

To me the most thrilling thing in the world is to give out the Word of God and to know that by His providence God will bring this one and that one to Himself.

How we should thank God for His providential dealings in the affairs of men! We can take this little Book of Esther and trace His hand through it all, although He is not visible in Person. The participants in this drama were totally unaware that God was directing; yet in every turn of events He was leading and guiding.

God has not taken His hand off this earth. It may seem as though He has, but He has not. Nor has He taken His hand off your life and mine. Whoever you are, God is moving in your life. I pray that you will recognize this, and that you will trust Christ as your Savior and your Guide.

# ·4·

## Haman and Anti-Semitism

*Esther, Chapter 3*

After these things did king Ahasuerus promote
Haman the son of Hammedatha the Agagite, and
advanced him, and set his seat above all the
princes that were with him. And all the king's
servants, that were in king's gate, bowed, and
reverenced Haman: for the king had so commanded concerning him. But Mordecai bowed
not, nor did him reverence. Then the king's servants, which were in the king's gate, said unto
Mordecai, Why transgressest thou the king's commandment? Now it came to pass, when they
spake daily unto him, and he hearkened not unto
them, that they told Haman, to see whether Mordecai's matters would stand: for he had told them
that he was a Jew. And when Haman saw that
Mordecai bowed not, nor did him reverence, then
was Haman full of wrath. And he thought scorn to
lay hands on Mordecai alone; for they had shewed
him the people of Mordecai: wherefore Haman

sought to destroy all the Jews that were throughout the whole kingdom of Ahasuerus, even the
people of Mordecai.

In the first month, that is, the month Nisan, in
the twelfth year of King Ahasuerus, they cast Pur,
that is, the lot, before Haman from day to day,
and from month to month, to the twelfth month,
that is, the month Adar.

And Haman said unto king Ahasuerus, There is
a certain people scattered abroad and dispersed
among the people in all the provinces of thy kingdom; and their laws are diverse from all people;
neither keep they the king's laws: therefore it is
not for the king's profit to suffer them. If it please
the king, let it be written that they may be destroyed: and I will pay ten thousand talents of
silver to the hands of those that have the charge of
the business, to bring it into the king's treasuries.
And the king took his ring from his hand, and
gave it unto Haman the son of Hammedatha the
Agagite, the Jews' enemy. And the king said unto
Haman, The silver is given to thee, the people
also, to do with them as it seemeth good to thee.
Then were the king's scribes called on the thirteenth day of the first month, and there was written according to all that Haman had commanded
unto the king's lieutenants, and to the governors
that were over every province, and to the rulers of
every people of every province according to the
writing thereof, and to every people after their
language; in the name of king Ahasuerus was it
written, and sealed with the king's ring. And the
letters were sent by posts into all the king's pro-

vinces, to destroy, to kill, and to cause to perish, all Jews, both young and old, little children and women, in one day, even upon the thirteenth day of the twelfth month, which is the month Adar, and to take the spoil of them for a prey. The copy of the writing for a commandment to be given in every province was published unto all people, that they should be ready against that day. The posts went out, being hastened by the king's commandment, and the decree was given in Shushan the palace. And the king and Haman sat down to drink; but the city Shushan was perplexed.

Chapter 3 introduces us to the man who truly is the villain of the Book of Esther: Haman. He had a bitterness and a hatred in his heart. He was identified as an Agagite. Does that suggest anything to you? In 1 Samuel 15 you'll find that Samuel told Saul that he was to exterminate the Amalekites (known also as Agagites). And you remember the disobedience of this man Saul; he did not do so. If Saul had done what God had commanded him to do, God's people would not have been threatened by Haman because the Agagites would have long before disappeared. God could see down through history and He knew what was coming. Saul's failure to exterminate the Agagites would have led to the extermination of his own people, but for the providence of God. Again, God is behind the scenes, keeping watch over His own.

Haman, apparently a very wealthy man, was promoted to a place next to Ahasuerus himself, the king of Persia. He was given a "blank check" signed by the king. He could have anything he wanted. He had free rein. And one of the things he required of the officials of the kingdom was to recognize his position and do obeisance to him. That is, they were to bow down to him.

As we have already seen, Mordecai was a judge at the gate. He had a political job, which meant he was one of the officials of the kingdom and he had to bow to Haman. However, Mordecai refused to bow. And for the first time, we see the hand of God beginning to move in the life of Mordecai. You may say, But he was out of the will of God. He should have returned to his own land. How could God move in a case like that?

These questions are appropriate. For reasons of his own, Mordecai did not return to Palestine, although that was his place. Clearly, he was out of the will of God; yet he still recognized God. Though Mordecai made no appeal to Him anywhere in the Book of Esther, it is evident he recognized God. How do I come to this conclusion? God's law to the Jews was explicit. They were not to bow to anything but God Himself. They were not to make an image, nor ever bow to an image. They were not to bow down to anything or anyone. So when Haman came by after his promotion, everybody who had a political job went down on their faces before him—except one man, Mordecai. Believe me, his lack of homage was obvious when he was the only one left standing!

The other officials ask him why he doesn't bow, and for the first time Mordecai reveals that he is a Jew. Up to this time he has told no one. You will remember that he had instructed Esther, when she entered the beauty contest, not to let anyone know her race. She did not even tell the king after they married.

But with Haman's promotion, Mordecai has to "let
the cat out of the bag," so to speak. He says flatly,
"The reason I'm not bowing is because I'm a Jew." The
minute he says that he also reveals his religion. He
worships only the true and living God; therefore he
bows to no idol, no image, no man. At this point in the
story I'm ready to throw my hat in the air and say,
"Hurrah for Mordecai!" For the first time, he is taking
a stand for God, and it is going to cost him a great deal.
I do not think he has any idea that the effects of his
declaration would be so far-reaching as to touch all of
his people, but he probably recognizes that it might
cost him his job and even his life.

As Mordecai began to stand out as a man of God,
Haman began to stand out in all his ugliness as a man
of Satan. The first thing we notice is his littleness. We
are going to note all the way through our study that
Haman is a little man. You'll hear him later on crying
on his wife's shoulder. He will say something like this:
"I've got everything in the world I want, and I can
have anything in the kingdom. But that little Jew
won't bow to me." Only a small man will let that sort
of thing bother him, and Haman permitted it to dis-
turb him a great deal.

In his agitation, Haman decided to do a terrible
thing. "And he thought scorn to lay hands on Morde-
cai alone; for they had shewed him the people of
Mordecai: wherefore Haman sought to destroy all the
Jews that were throughout the whole kingdom of
Ahasuerus, even the people of Mordecai" (3:6).

Haman did not know, I am sure, anything about the
promise that God had made to Abraham. When God
called Abraham, He said to him:

> And I will make of thee a great nation, and I will bless thee, and make thy name great; and thou shalt be a blessing: And I will bless them that bless thee, and curse him that curseth thee: and in thee shall all families of the earth be blessed (Gen. 12:2,3).

God has made that promise good. Whether you and I like it or not, all we have to do is turn back the pages of history, and we'll find that every great nation has persecuted the descendants of Abraham—the Jews—and has tried to exterminate them. Yet the Jews have attended the funeral of every one of these great nations. More recently, Hitler tried to exterminate them in the ovens and in the camps of the Gestapo. He thought he would get rid of them; yet today Hitler and his group are gone, and the Jews are still with us.

It is not likely that either Hitler or Haman—or contemporary anti-Semites—are cognizant of or pay much attention to Isaiah 54:17. But anyone who is tinctured with anti-Semitism ought to read this:

> No weapon that is formed against thee shall prosper; and every tongue that shall rise against thee in judgment thou shalt condemn. This is the heritage of the servants of the LORD, and their righteousness is of me, saith the LORD.

God says that He will take care of every instrument that is formed to destroy this people. No people have ever been abused by the nations of the world as have the Jews. That they have not been exterminated is in itself miraculous. God has preserved them. And we will see Him do it in the Book of Esther.

Haman's irritation grows every time he goes through the gate. All the people go down on their face except that little Jew Mordecai, and it disturbs him. He resolves to do something about it. Finally, he takes the liberty of going to Ahasuerus himself. He says, "There is a people in your kingdom who are different, and they are causing trouble." And Ahasuerus has so little regard for life, as most of the potentates of that day did, that he does not even inquire who the people happen to be. Haman does not know that Esther the queen happens to belong to that nationality. Even Ahasuerus himself does not know that his queen is Jewish, nor does he know that he is signing away her life at this time. He takes a ring off his finger, and he gives it to Haman. It is his signet ring. The signet on the ring, pressed down in soft wax, becomes the signature of the king. An order that had that signet stamped on it would become the law of the kingdom. So Ahasuerus carelessly takes off his ring, hands it to Haman, and says in effect, "I don't know who they are and I don't care who they are, but if you feel they ought to be exterminated, then go ahead and take care of the matter." What little regard Ahasuerus has for human life!

The decree now goes out as a law of the Medes and Persians. "Then were the king's scribes called on the thirteenth day of the first month, and there was written according to all that Haman had commanded unto the king's lieutenants, and to the governors that were over every province, and to the rulers of every people of every province according to the writing thereof, and to every people after their language; in the name of king Ahasuerus was it written, and sealed with the king's ring" (3:12).

And this was the content of the message that went

out: "And the letters were sent by posts into all the king's provinces, to destroy, to kill, and to cause to perish, all Jews, both young and old, little children and women, in one day, even upon the thirteenth day of the twelfth month, which is the month Adar, and to take the spoil of them for a prey" (3:13).

On a certain day the Jews were to be exterminated. Haman was giving anti-Semitism full rein and permitting a great many to do what apparently was in their hearts. On this designated day murdering Jews would be legal.

Haman's decree is a chapter in the life of the Jew that has been duplicated many, many times. When you read this chapter, you can almost substitute the name of Pharaoh or Hitler or Nasser for Haman. In fact, there are many names that would fit here. There never has been a time since the Israelites became a nation down in the land of Egypt that there has not been a movement somewhere to exterminate them. As I write this, the Jews in Russia are under awful persecution. Russia will permit only certain ones to come out and return to Palestine; there are actually ample funds available for this purpose.

Notice that Haman's decree was to go out into all the provinces, which means that the Jews were scattered all over the Medo-Persian Empire. That empire covered two continents and had even penetrated into Europe. The Jews had been scattered throughout the civilized world because of the Babylonian captivity.

Evidently there was a wave of anti-Semitism throughout the entire Persian kingdom. And the thing that precipitated it as far as Haman was concerned was one Jew, Mordecai.

The decree went out as a law of the Medes and Persians. We were told again and again at the very beginning of this book that a law once made was irrevocable. The law could not be changed, nor could it be repealed. The law had to stand on the books. "The posts went out, being hastened by the king's commandment, and the decree was given in Shushan the palace. And the king and Haman sat down to drink; but the city Shushan was perplexed" (3:15). The people in the city could not understand what was happening. Although they may not have liked the Jews, and although they considered them foreigners with differing customs in their midst, most of them did not want to exterminate them. They were perplexed. They could not understand Ahasuerus permitting a decree like this to go out. But Ahasuerus and Haman sat down to drink over it.

Outside Shushan the palace late that evening you could see the riders getting their orders. Literally hundreds of them must have been pressed into service because this was a great kingdom with many provinces. The different riders were given copies of the new decree that had become law. One company started riding down the road to the south; one went to the north; another to the west; a fourth to the east. They rode all night. When they came to a little town, they nailed on the bulletin board of that town the decree for the people to read the next morning. Then the riders pressed on. When their horses tired, fresh horses were there to carry on. All over the kingdom, the decree was posted, the decree that the Jews were to perish. The messengers hastened, we are told, at the king's commandment.

Anti-Semitism is an awful thing—and it's with us today. Certainly no Christian should have any part in it.

Anti-Semitism had its origin down in the brickyards of Egypt, under the cruel hands of Pharaoh, where the Jews became a nation. From that time on the great nations of the world have moved against them. It was the story of Assyria and it was the story of Babylon, the nations that took them into captivity. In the Book of Esther we see how the Jews fared in Persia. Rome also must plead guilty, and the Spanish Inquisition was leveled largely at the Jews. Under Hitler in Germany it is estimated that six million Jews perished.

What is the reason for this persecution that we call anti-Semitism? Let's analyze it briefly. There are two things that are back of it. The first reason is a natural one; the second, supernatural.

The natural reason is simply this: The Jews are unlovely. Now do not misunderstand me. There was a Christian Jew in Memphis, Tennessee, who was a very personal friend of mine. Some years ago as I was holding a series of meetings there, he came to me and said, "Mac, there is a spirit of anti-Semitism rising in Memphis and throughout this part of America. I find it on every hand. Some people are attempting to foment it and stir it up in this country." Then he added, with bowed head, "My people give cause for it. They are so unlovely at times." Before agreeing with him, let's face the fact: Any godless person, Jew or Gentile, is unlovely. I know of no person more unlovely than a godless Gentile, nor do I know a lovelier person than a Christian Jew. God sees us unlovely, undone, and unattractive, but by His sovereign grace He makes us new creatures in Christ. That same grace reached down and called the Israelites God's chosen people.

There is also a supernatural reason that the Jews are hated. In the providence and design of God, the people of this race have been designated the custodians of His written Word. The Bible has come to us through them. God chose them for that. They transmitted the Scriptures. Satan hates them because they have been the repository of the Scriptures and because the Lord Jesus Christ, after the flesh, came from them—as Paul put it: "Whose are the fathers, and of whom as concerning the flesh Christ came . . ." (Rom. 9:5). There is no way of escaping the fact that there is a supernatural hatred of them, in part because Jesus was born a Jew. This is certainly clear in Scripture. And we know that God has chosen the Jewish race as His people, as His nation. Several years ago a wag wrote the following words on a bulletin board:

> It is odd
> That God
> Should choose
> The Jew.

A Jew came and wrote underneath it:

> God chose,
> Which shows
> God knew
> His Jew.

A Christian came along and wrote beneath that:

> This Jew
> Spoke true.
> God knew
> His Jew

As King
Would bring
To earth
New birth.

God chose them for that purpose, and because of that they are hated. They are hated by Satan, and as a result the nations of the world are fanned into fury at times against these people.

There is, by the way, a very subtle form of anti-Semitism in our midst today: Denying that all of the promises made to the nation Israel by God will be fulfilled. A very eminent scholar said to me recently, "I do not like your Judaistic eschatology." He also used another term for it, namely "Scofieldism." He continued, "I do not like this idea that God has yet to deal with the nation of Israel." I told him that I consider that the very heart of the Bible. Then I asked him what he did with the promises made to Israel. He said, "They are for the church." Immediately I asked, "What about the curses that were pronounced on the nation Israel?" "Well," he said, "I don't worry with those." Never yet have I found anyone who takes the promises away from Israel that ever takes the curses also! They always leave the curses for the Jews. Beloved, they have the curses, but they have the promises too.

Here is one of the promises concerning the Jews:

Thus saith the LORD, which giveth the sun for a light by day, and the ordinances of the moon and of the stars for a light by night, which divideth the sea when the waves thereof roar; The LORD of hosts is his name: If those ordinances depart from before me, saith the LORD, then the seed of Israel also shall cease from being a nation before me for ever (Jer. 31:35,36).

Think of that! God says that if you can blot the sun out
of the sky, if you can wipe the moon out of existence,
then you can get rid of the nation of Israel. But as long
as the sun shines and the moon is in the heavens, God
says that He is not through with these people. They
are His chosen instrument.

Had it not been for God's faithfulness to His promises, these people would have been obliterated from
the face of the earth at the time of Queen Esther. God
ever stands in the shadows, keeping watch over His
own.

# ·5·

## For Such a Time as This

*Esther, Chapter 4*

When Mordecai perceived all that was done, Mordecai rent his clothes, and put on sackcloth with ashes, and went out into the midst of the city, and cried with a loud and a bitter cry; and came even before the king's gate: for none might enter into the king's gate clothed with sackcloth. And in every province, whithersoever the king's commandment and his decree came, there was great mourning among the Jews, and fasting, and weeping, and wailing; and many lay in sackcloth and ashes.

So Esther's maids and her chamberlains came and told it her. Then was the queen exceedingly grieved; and she sent raiment to clothe Mordecai, and to take away his sackcloth from him, but he received it not. Then called Esther for Hatach, one of the king's chamberlains, whom he had appointed to attend upon her, and gave him a commandment to Mordecai, to know what it was, and why it was. So Hatach went forth to Mordecai unto the street of the city, which was before the king's gate. And Mordecai told him of all that had happened unto him, and of the sum of the money that Haman had promised to pay to the king's treasuries for the Jews, to destroy them. Also he gave him the copy of the writing of the decree that was given at Shushan to destroy them, to shew it unto Esther, and to declare it unto her, and to charge her that she should go in unto the king, to make supplication unto him, and to make request before him for her people. And Hatach came and told Esther the words of Mordecai.

Again Esther spoke unto Hatach, and gave him commandment unto Mordecai; All the king's servants, and the people of the king's provinces, do know, that whosoever, whether man or woman, shall come unto the king into the inner court, who is not called, there is one law of his to put him to death, except such to whom the king shall hold out the golden sceptre, that he may live: but I have not been called to come in unto the king these thirty days. And they told to Mordecai Esther's words. Then Mordecai commanded to answer Esther, Think not with thyself that thou shalt escape in the king's house, more than all the Jews. For if thou altogether holdest thy peace at this time, then shall there enlargement and deliverance arise to the Jews from another place; but thou and thy father's house shall be destroyed: and who knoweth whether thou art come to the kingdom for such a time as this?

Then Esther bade them return to Mordecai this

answer, Go, gather together all the Jews that are present in Shushan, and fast ye for me, and neither eat nor drink three days, night or day: I also and my maidens will fast likewise; and so will I go in unto the king, which is not according to the law: and if I perish, I perish. So Mordecai went his way, and did according to all that Esther had commanded him.

Chapter 4 of Esther opens with the reaction of Mordecai to what had happened, along with the reaction in every province. "And in every province, whithersoever the king's commandment and his decree came, there was great mourning among the Jews, and fasting, and weeping, and wailing; and many lay in sackcloth and ashes" (4:3). Do you notice that there was no call to prayer? These people were out of the will of God. As was said earlier, the decree of Cyrus, prophesied by Isaiah, had permitted them to return to Israel, but these folk did not return. They were out of God's will, and consequently they made no call to prayer whatsoever. Yet they went through the remainder of the ritual: fasting, putting on the sackcloth and ashes, and mourning greatly.

The Jews *believed* the decree that had gone out from Ahasuerus. It was the law of the Medes and the Persians, which was unalterable according to these historical books and also according to the Book of Daniel. And you remember that even Xerxes himself, when he had put aside his beautiful queen Vashti, could never take her again because the decree had been made that she was to come no more before the king. Even he could not change his own law after it had been made.

So when this decree of death came throughout the empire, the Jews believed it and mourned in sackcloth and ashes.

It is a strange and sad commentary upon the human race that, although from the throne of God, there had to come a decree to this world that "All have sinned, and come short of the glory of God" (Rom. 3:23) and "The wages of sin is death" (Rom. 6:23), there are those today who treat this as if it were not true at all. The average person you meet on the street will tell you that he does not believe this. How foolish it would have been if the Jews in that day had not believed that the decree of death would be enforced. Yet almighty God says that ". . . death passed upon all men, for that all have sinned" (Rom. 5:12). He also says, "It is appointed unto men once to die, but after this the judgment" (Heb. 9:27).

Conspicuously absent today (and the church, I think, is responsible) is conviction concerning sin—not only in the hearts and lives of the unsaved but also in the hearts and lives of believers. The average believer says, "Yes, I trust Christ," but he has no real conviction of sin in his life at all. It is absent in contemporary church life. When is the last time you heard a sinner, either a saved sinner or a lost sinner, cry out to God for mercy? At the beginning of my ministry I used to see a great many tears, and I used to see people cry out to God. I do not see that today. Even in evangelistic crusades there is a great deal of "coming forward," but there is that lack of weeping over sin in the lives of folk. Why? They just don't believe God means it. They do not believe that sin merits punishment. They do not believe that God intends to enforce judgment against sin and against the sinner who holds to it and will not turn to Christ.

Mordecai knew and believed the seriousness of the decree. "When Mordecai perceived all that was done, Mordecai rent his clothes, and put on sackcloth with ashes, and went out into the midst of the city, and cried with a loud and bitter cry" (4:1).

However, Esther, living in safety and seclusion in the queen's quarters, knew nothing of the decree. She did not realize what was taking place until her maids and her chamberlains came to tell her that her cousin Mordecai was in sackcloth and ashes. Perhaps she thought, *That's not a very nice way to show his appreciation for my getting him this very excellent position as judge—by mourning in sackcloth and ashes!*

". . . Then was the queen exceedingly grieved; and she sent raiment to clothe Mordecai, and to take away his sackcloth from him: but he received it not" (4:4). She thought, *I don't know what the trouble is, but I'm going to send him some colorful clothes.* She sent a sporty new suit, something very ornate. But he turned it away. Why? Because it wasn't new clothes that he needed. Esther, secure in the palace, thought that all in the world Mordecai needed was a new suit of clothes to make him take off the sackcloth and ashes. But gaudy clothes could not destroy the terrible edict of death. Mordecai did not regard the clothes as having any part in the grave crisis, so he refused them.

Today there are a great many folk who are wearing gaudy garments. They refuse to believe that we are all sinners, although God has declared that we are. They reach out for any garment that might hide from them the reality of sin.

The fact of the matter is, there are those today who take the position that sin is actually only a mistake or an error. There is one word in the Bible for that, *hamartano*, meaning "to miss the mark." It means, actually, to take an arrow, put it in a bow, pull it back, let the arrow fly, but come short of the bull's-eye. A great many people today think that is the extent of sin. It is just to miss the mark. It is a mistake, an error. You just say, "Pardon me," and go on. That's all in the world that sin is, and God has no right to hold us responsible for our mistakes. If we say, "Pardon me," He ought to say, "I pardon you." And that ends it.

There are also those today who take that position and think all the human family needs is reformation. There are a great many religions today—a great many cults—that go in for reformation. As I write, members of the Hollywood movie colony are falling over each other to get to these Indian gurus. They go to them because they are trying to find some program whereby they can improve themselves, reform themselves, or change themselves. They argue that sinning man has only blundered and needs nothing but the gaudy garments of a few reformation programs. Oh, for the understanding of Mordecai! He knew that only the garments of sackcloth and ashes are proper raiment when facing the reality of sin.

There is another type of garment in which people take refuge: education. In the 1920s that was the method. Shaler Matthews, who in that day was connected with the University of Chicago's School of Religion, gave this definition of sin: "Sin is the backward pull of an outworn good." Think that one over for a while. Take away the modifiers and what you have left is "Sin is good." Some readers can remember the twenties, when it was taught that all we had to do was educate folk. If we would educate them right, we would get rid of this thing called sin, since it was nothing but selfishness.

I had such an experience when a Christian day school was begun in the church where I served as pastor. The principal came into my study one day and said, "Dr. McGee, I have a case that I don't know what to do with."

I asked, "What in the world is it?"

"Well," she said, "a mother from one of the liberal churches has brought over a child. She wants to get him out of the public school and into a Christian school, but apparently she has misunderstood what a Christian school is."

The mother had talked to the principal in the presence of the child. When she came to the word *sin* she did not pronounce it; instead she spelled it out. The same thing occurred when she came to the word D-e-v-i-l. She insisted that she did not want the little fellow to hear those words, as they belonged to the Dark Ages.

The principal asked me what she should do. I said, "Well, I think I'd tell the mother that it's better for the little boy to find out about s-i-n and D-e-v-i-l in a Christian day school than to find out about them written on the back fence in an alley. I don't think that is the best way to be educated. If she thinks that her little Willy is going to grow up in this world without knowing what sin is and who the Devil is, then she certainly is living in a dream world herself and needs to move into a world of reality."

We need more than education. People cannot be educated away from sin. Right now some of the biggest sinners abroad are carrying Ph.D. degrees.

There are those who have attempted to define sin as ignorance. That is, since people don't know the way and must find the way, they must "discover" God. There is a great deal of that going on right now. People are attempting to discover God. When I was speaking in the San Francisco Bay area several months ago, a young man told me one evening, "I have been interested in what you have had to say tonight because I am trying to discover God. I heard that you were over here, and I thought I might get a new angle."

"Did you get a new angle tonight?" I asked him.

"Yes, I got a new angle."

And that is about all he got, because he was attempting to *find* a way. People become religious today because of that. They say they are turning to God.

I have come to the conclusion that the increase in church membership after World War II was merely an escape mechanism for a great many folk. It was like a life insurance policy; joining the church was an escape from God. You may say to me, "That is strange reasoning." I don't think so. People found that if they joined the church, they became insulated from any type of evangelism. If anyone asked them if they were a Christian, they could immediately say, "I'm a Presbyterian," or "I'm a Methodist," or "I'm a Baptist," or "I'm a member of such-and-such a church." You can be all of that and not be saved, my beloved. These are garments that people have attempted to put on—gaudy garments—but they do not cancel the edict that has gone out from the throne of God that we are all sinners and that sin must be dealt with.

Although the great difference between liberal and conservative theology has been on the doctrine of the Lord Jesus Christ and His deity, the final test is attitude toward sin. Let a person tell you what he or she thinks about sin, and you know what that person thinks about Christ. Because of the impact and influence of liberalism, many people have lost a consciousness of sin. The average definition of a Christian today is one who lives a respectable life in the community and stays out of jail. (By this definition the apostle Paul would not qualify because he saw the jails from the inside throughout the Roman Empire!) No, just to be moralists does not mean that we are Christians. All have sinned; all stand in His presence as lost sinners.

Samuel Johnson, England's great literary critic of the eighteenth century, made this observation: "Every man knows that of himself which he dares not tell his dearest friend." Goethe, the German author, said: "I never read of a crime that has been committed but that I, too, might have committed." Remember this: You and I have the same kind of nature as every other individual walking the face of the earth. "But," you say, "I would not commit that crime!" Of course you would not, but do you know why? It is because of the grace of God. We are all sinners in the sight of God. That is His condemnation. And no one has anything to present to God for salvation.

Others complain, "You always emphasize that we are all sinners." The reason I emphasize that fact is because I find that it is not being emphasized in our society. A young man in my own congregation once was very resentful. In fact, he was angry.

"Dr. McGee," he said, "I resent your saying that we

all are sinners. I take it that you are referring to my mother as a sinner."

"Yes," I said, "you inferred correctly."

"Well," he said, "I want you to know that I have the loveliest mother, the most wonderful mother . . ." and tears rolled down the boy's cheeks. "My mother is not a sinner."

"Have you ever stopped to think about this," I replied. "David thought a great deal of his mother, but in Psalm 51:5 David said, 'In sin did my mother conceive me.' Have you turned that over in your mind?" He turned and walked out.

All of us have sinned and come short of the glory of God. This morning a beautiful young lady came to my associate pastor and demanded, "Why is Dr. McGee so negative? Why does he emphasize our being sinners?" She did not like it. "Why doesn't he talk about the good and the beautiful? Why does he emphasize sin?" She agreed to have an interview with the pastor, and I hope she will find that the reason I emphasize sin is that sin is common to the human family and that she is a sinner and needs a Savior.

Some folk ask me, "Are people worse today than they were years ago?" Frankly, I do not think so. There is not more sin in the world today, there is just no consciousness of sin so that sin is out in the open. A man on television the other night frankly said that he was a homosexual. Twenty years ago, that man never would have opened his mouth on that subject. You see, what used to be done in the back yard is now done in the front yard. What used to be done under-cover is now being done out in the open. People have been sinners right down through the ages, but it is the consciousness of sin that we have lost today.

Mordecai could have put on the gaudy garments Esther sent to him and ignored the decree that had gone out, but that would not have changed the fact that he was a Jew and that on a certain date he was to die. He and the rest of the Jews would have been absolutely stupid not to believe it.

The gaudy garments of religion or reformation or education will not cover our nakedness before the holy presence of God. The fig leaves were not adequate for our first parents; they had to be clothed with that which God provided. Not only will Christ forgive our sins, but He will clothe us in the robe of His righteousness, giving us an eternal standing before God (see Rev. 19:8). Do not take the garments which the world offers. Only the robe of righteousness can cover your sin before a holy and just God.

Mordecai sends a message back to Queen Esther saying to her in effect, "The reason that I'm in sackcloth and ashes is that our people, you and I, have come under an awful decree of death." And Esther sends back a message to him to this effect, "That's too bad. I'm sorry to hear it. I didn't know about it before." And she adds, ". . . but I have not been called to come in unto the king these thirty days" (4:11). That is to say, "I do not know his attitude toward me—and you know what the law is."

As was the case in every kingdom of that day, anyone who dared go into the presence of the king without being summoned would be summarily and automatically put to death, unless the king extended his sceptre to him. Ahasuerus was noted for his fits of temper; he could have put his queen to death if she had gone in without being called. So Esther sends word back to Mordecai, "If I go in, it may mean death

to me." Then Mordecai returns to her this memorable
message: ". . . Think not with thyself that thou shalt
escape in the king's house, more than all the Jews"
(4:13). "Just because you happen to be the queen does
not exempt you from the execution, because it will
reach every Jew in the kingdom, and it'll reach the
queen."

Mordecai goes on to say, "For if thou altogether
holdest thy peace at this time, then shall there enlargement and deliverance arise to the Jews from another
place . . ." (4:14). Someday when I see Mordecai (and I
do expect to see him), I'd like to ask him what he had
in mind when he said that deliverance would arise
from another place. I've thought this over, and I ask
you the question: What other place was there to which
they could turn? Where could deliverance have come
to them except from God? He was their only hope at
this time, and I'm confident that Mordecai had that in
mind when he said, "If *you* don't move, then deliverance will come from another place." God would move
in another direction. Mordecai must have known that
deliverance would come because he was acquainted
with the promises that God had made to Abraham. So
he challenges his cousin, ". . . who knoweth whether
thou art come to the kingdom for such a time as this?"
(4:14).

We begin to see God by His providence moving now
in the affairs of the nation. It is obvious that Esther did
not accidentally win the beauty contest. She was not
accidentally the one who became queen. She was in
her position for a very definite purpose, and God had
been arranging this all the time. "Who knoweth
whether thou art come to the kingdom for such a time

as this?" What a challenge was given to this young woman, and God used her. If she had not moved, God would have moved in a different direction. But she was placed there for a purpose.

Have you ever noticed how the hand of God has moved in the affairs of this world and that "at such a time as this" God has brought certain ones to the kingdom? Let me remind you of several. Abraham was called of God in a day when the whole world seemed to be departing from God as it had in the days of Noah. God called this man to move out, and through him He brought the Savior into the world. He came to the kingdom for such a time as that. Moses was a man who stood in the gap. He was the one God raised up at a particular time to be the deliverer of his people. Then there was David. While Saul, Satan's man, was plunging the nation into sin and idolatry, God was training a shepherd boy to be the king. David came to the kingdom for such a time as that.

John the Baptist, a solo voice crying in the wilderness, the first voice lifted in God's behalf after a silence of four hundred years, was called to the kingdom for such a time as that.

Saul of Tarsus was a brilliant young man who hated Christ and the church, but God all the time was training him, for he was to come to the kingdom for such a time.

Luther, Calvin, John Knox, John Wesley were raised up by God. Lloyd George said that Wesley was the greatest man who ever lived. He made the greatest contribution to England. These were men whom God raised up.

Let's move to the secular realm. I noticed in World

War II that God seemed to be moving. Can you remember the day when Hitler was coming to power?
Can you remember when he was having victory after
victory, and he overran France? He was moving into
Russia; he was moving through North Africa. But God
raised up a Christian general by the name of Mont-
gomery. He is the one who started the wave that
halted the progress of this awful Nazi horde. Isn't it
interesting that God also raised up in the Far East
General Douglas MacArthur at the right time?

Isn't it interesting that God has *not* raised up a man
in this day? That ought to make America come alert.
During my entire ministry I have been looking for God
to raise up somebody to lead America back to God.
The first time Billy Graham ever spoke in Los Angeles,
I said, "Maybe this is the man." Now God has used
him marvelously, but Billy himself says he has not
seen revival. I'm wondering if somewhere God may be
training some young boy, some young man. Wouldn't
it be wonderful if God would raise up some young
person today through whom He could bring real revival to America?

You may say, "You're a premillennialist, and you
believe the apostasy is on us, so it's impossible to have
a revival!" Nothing is impossible with God. I believe
that God, by His providence, could be training and
bringing up someone for such a time as this.

Oh, beloved, this is an hour when God's people
must pray that He will set apart a man for clear and
powerful leadership in a revival, for revival will come
through a human instrument. Ask God for this man.

Naturally, some are going to say, "Yes, but you are
speaking of great folk. We are little people, and God

does not move in our affairs like that." Oh, but you can be great in prayer and faithful in giving out the Word in your small sphere. Think of the Scottish minister (whose name we do not even know) who gave his report to the elders at the end of one year. They had prayer and great heart-searching and concluded that the year had been a complete failure. There had been only one conversion: wee Bobby Moffat. Can you imagine having the privilege of humbly leading to Christ such a man as Robert Moffat, the great missionary to Africa? That was the greatest work for God that minister ever did; yet he confessed it as his greatest failure.

God moves strangely in the affairs of this world. Let us take a hypothetical case in examining ourselves with reference to this fact. You may be a young person who has heard a soul-stirring message by a missionary from the mountains of Kentucky. Perhaps you are much impressed; you feel the call of God to go to Kentucky, while the person sitting next to you is not interested. Suppose in those mountains there is a little boy who, in the economy of God, is going to be President of these United States. Suppose you refuse the call of God and stay home instead. Suppose that little fellow grows up, becomes a godless young man, and when he is elected to the presidency of the United States, he brings this nation to destruction and defeat. I ask you, without answering the question, because I don't know the answer: Who is responsible? Too few of us are concerned about fitting our lives into God's great plan and purpose. "Thou art come to the kingdom for such a time as this."

Watch Esther. She is a queen now, every inch a

queen. She says simply, ". . . if I perish, I perish" (4:16). What a statement! How noble she becomes.

Her statement reminds us of Another who said, "For even the Son of man came not to be ministered unto, but to minister, and to give his life a ransom for many" (Mark 10:45). Christ also said, ". . . I lay down my life, that I might take it again. No man taketh it from me, but I lay it down of myself. I have power to lay it down, and I have power to take it again . . ." (John 10:17,18). This One came to our earth; He gave His life a ransom for many. He came from heaven's glory to perish—to die upon the cross so that you and I might be saved.

During the Civil War the last and the bloodiest battle occurred when Grant surrounded Richmond. The two armies moved back and forth over the battlements all day long. At times it looked as if the boys in gray would win, and then all odds seemed to be in favor of the boys in blue. The battlefield was strewn with the wounded, the dying, the dead. In the intense heat of the afternoon the cry began to go up, "Water . . . water . . . water." Finally, a young lieutenant could stand it no longer, and he went to his commanding officer for permission to carry water to those men. He filled his canteen from the canteens of the others around him, and he crawled across the battlefield between the firing lines. He went first to one man and then to another giving them water. Finally the boys in blue as well as the boys in gray saw him. The commanders on both sides called for a halt, there was a cease-fire, and a shout went up from both sides as this young lieutenant went from man to man bringing water.

That was a brave act.

Beloved, there is One more noble than that. He vaulted the battlements of heaven, came down to earth, and took upon Himself our human flesh. He didn't say, "If I perish, I perish." He said, "I came to *give* my life a ransom for many."

# · 6 ·

## *When a King Could Not Sleep*

*Esther, Chapters 5:1-6:4*

Now it came to pass on the third day, that
Esther put on her royal apparel, and stood in the
inner court of the king's house, over against the
king's house: and the king sat upon his royal
throne in the royal house, over against the gate of
the house. And it was so, when the king saw
Esther the queen standing in the court, that she
obtained favour in his sight: and the king held out
to Esther the golden sceptre that was in his hand.
So Esther drew near, and touched the top of the
sceptre. Then said the king unto her, What wilt
thou, Queen Esther? and what is thy request? it
shall be even given thee to the half of the kingdom. And Esther answered, If it seem good unto
the king, let the king and Haman come this day
unto the banquet that I have prepared for him.
Then the king said, Cause Haman to make haste,
that he may do as Esther hath said. So the king
and Haman came to the banquet that Esther had
prepared.

And the king said unto Esther at the banquet of wine, What is thy petition? and it shall be granted thee: and what is thy request? even to the half of the kingdom it shall be performed. Then answered Esther, and said, My petition and my request is; If I have found favour in the sight of the king, and if it please the king to grant my petition, and to perform my request, let the king and Haman come to the banquet that I shall prepare for them, and I will do to-morrow as the king hath said.

Then went Haman forth that day joyful and with a glad heart: but when Haman saw Mordecai in the king's gate, that he stood not up, nor moved for him, he was full of indignation against Mordecai. Nevertheless Haman refrained himself: and when he came home, he sent and called for his friends, and Zeresh his wife. And Haman told them of the glory of his riches, and the multitude of his children, and all the things wherein the king had promoted him, and how he had advanced him above the princes and servants of the king. Haman said moreover, Yea, Esther the queen did let no man come in with the king unto the banquet that she had prepared but myself; and to-morrow am I invited unto her also with the king. Yet all this availeth me nothing, so long as I see Mordecai the Jew sitting at the king's gate.

Then said Zeresh his wife and all his friends unto him, Let a gallows be made of fifty cubits high, and to-morrow speak thou unto the king that Mordecai may be hanged thereon: then go thou in merrily with the king unto the banquet. And the thing pleased Haman; and he caused the gallows to be made.

On that night could not the king sleep, and he commanded to bring the book of records of the chronicles; and they were read before the king. And it was found written, that Mordecai had told of Bigthana and Teresh, two of the king's chamberlains, the keepers of the door, who sought to lay hand on the king Ahasuerus. And the king said, What honour and dignity hath been done to Mordecai for this? Then said the king's servants that ministered unto him, There is nothing done for him.

And the king said, Who is in the court? Now Haman was come into the outward court of the king's house, to speak unto the king to hang Mordecai on the gallows that he had prepared for him.

Picking up the narrative where the preceding chapter ended, we see that the brave Queen Esther agreed that, for the sake of her people, she would go into the presence of the king to plead for them. You understand that when she entered the beauty contest Mordecai had instructed her not to tell anything about her nationality—that she was a Jewess. Her race was still unknown to the king when he signed the decree, having been paid a large sum of money by Haman to exterminate the Jews in the kingdom of Persia. And of course, practically all of the Jews were in that kingdom in that day so that it would have meant the total extermination of these people. Esther's mission was a most important one.

The custom of the day was that no one could come into the presence of the king unless the king asked for him or her. If a person dared to come into his presence uninvited, and he did not extend to him or her his sceptre, it would mean death. Ahasuerus did not even have to move. If he simply sat without lifting his sceptre, the person who had entered would be taken out and summarily executed with neither trial nor questions asked. The king was supreme, of course.

Notice that in this hour of crisis Esther did not ask that her people be in prayer. She asked for the Jews to fast (4:16), but she did not mention prayer. After all, they were out of the will of God, and God's name is not even mentioned in this book. But God is standing in the shadows here, keeping watch over His own. This is my reason for believing that the purpose of this book in the canon of Scripture is to teach the providence of God. The hand of God is in the glove of history. Though men may neither recognize Him nor acknowledge Him, He is moving in the affairs of the world.

Esther turned to preparing herself for appearing before the king. You will remember that the first time she had come before the king and had won the beauty contest, she had required none of the fine clothing or elaborate accessories that the other contestants had used. By her natural beauty she had won, and the king had fallen in love with her. But this time I'm sure that she spent a great deal of time on her dress. We are told that "Esther put on her royal apparel" (5:1), which meant that she put on the finest that she had. It meant that she looked the best that she could. In fact, if I may use the language of the street, she knocked the king's eye out! I tell you, she was lovely.

"And it was so, when the king saw Esther the queen standing in the court, that she obtained favour in his

sight: and the king held out to Esther the golden sceptre that was in his hand. So Esther drew near, and
touched the top of the sceptre" (5:2).

When she steps into that royal court and waits—it is
certainly a dramatic moment—the king looks at her.
Will he raise the sceptre or will he not? In this moment
I'm confident this Hebrew girl prays, although there is
no record of it. She must recognize how helpless and
hopeless she really is. Then the king holds out the
golden sceptre to her, and possibly smiles. She ad-
vances and places her hand on the sceptre, as was the
custom of the day.

What a picture we have here! In this book I have
been emphasizing the law of the Medes and Persians
and comparing their law to the law of God. God's law
says, "The soul that sinneth, it shall die" (Ezek. 18:20).
God has never changed that. It is as true now as it ever
was that the soul that sins shall die. That's God's law.
It is immutable. He cannot change that without changing His character.

There is another side to the story. Just as the king
held out the sceptre to Queen Esther, our God holds
out the sceptre to humanity today. It is true that "All
have sinned and come short of the glory of God"
(Rom. 3:23). It is true we are "dead in trespasses and
sins" (Eph. 2:1). It is true that "The soul that sinneth, it
shall die." But our God overcame that tremendous
law, and the only way in the world He could overcome
it was for Him to come to this earth Himself, take upon
Himself our sins, and pay that penalty. The law was
not abrogated, and it is not abrogated today. When
God saves you, it is because Somebody else paid the
penalty for your sins. Jesus died a substitutionary

death upon that cross for you and me. As a result of that, God holds out to the earth the sceptre of grace, and He says to an individual, "You can come to Me. You can touch that sceptre of grace. You can receive from Me salvation because I am reconciled to you."

When Adam sinned in the Garden of Eden, he lost his fellowship with God. I do not mean to be irreverent, but I think God lost more than Adam lost. God lost His fellowship also with this creature whom He evidently had created for fellowship. They were together at the beginning; God came down and had fellowship with Adam. Then Adam rebelled against God and sinned. When Adam sinned, he turned his back on God, and a holy God must turn His back on a sinner.

But when Christ died on the cross, God turned around. Paul said to the Corinthian believers, "We are ambassadors for Christ" (2 Cor. 5:20), and you never have an ambassador unless there is peace between the two countries. The embassy is closed when there is war, and the ambassador goes home. God is not at war with this world today. Let me paraphrase what Paul said: "We are His ambassadors down here, and we are saying, 'Be *ye* reconciled to God' " (2 Cor. 5:20).

The gospel is simply this: God is favorable; His sceptre of grace is extended to you, and He's asking you simply to turn around. Will you turn around? God holds out the sceptre of grace to a lost world. The message of His ambassador is, "Be ye reconciled to God." Notice that you don't have to reconcile God; He is already reconciled. That happened when Christ died on the cross.

When Esther comes into the presence of the king, he

recognizes immediately that she never would have been so bold if an emergency had not arisen. Notice how he speaks to her: "Then said the king unto her, What wilt thou, queen Esther? and what is thy request?" (5:3). He uses the expression "It shall be even given thee to the half of the kingdom" (5:3). This is no idle expression. He means that he sees she is greatly distressed, and he wants to make her feel comfortable. So he puts into her hand a blank check. "Whatever your request is, up to half the kingdom, it's yours. You fill out the check."

"And Esther answered, If it seem good unto the king, let the king and Haman come this day unto the banquet that I have prepared for him" (5:4). This is a remarkable verse in several respects. Notice a technical detail that may be important. As you have seen, the name of God is not in the Book of Esther, but this verse in the Hebrew forms an acrostic, and that acrostic is the name of God, which is quite interesting indeed. There are those who believe it was put here for that very reason. I do not know.

The verse also tells us something about Esther. This girl did not make her request known at first. She wanted Haman present when she let the king know that what he had demanded was not only the death of the Jews but her death also. "Then the king said, Cause Haman to make haste, that he may do as Esther hath said. . ." (5:5). In other words, "You tell Haman that Esther has invited us to dinner and that he is to come." And notice: "That he may do as Esther hath said."

The feeling of the king is evident here. He had been very generous to Haman. He had made him prime minister; he had given him his ring; he had let him send out the edict to slay the Jews; but when the comparison was made with Queen Esther, Haman had to obey her. Esther was queen, and she was in a very favorable light indeed.

". . . So the king and Haman came to the banquet that Esther had prepared" (5:5). At the banquet Esther obviously is anxious, so that Ahasuerus can see that something is troubling her a great deal. "And the king said unto Esther at the banquet of wine, What is thy petition? and it shall be granted thee: and what is thy request? even to the half of the kingdom it shall be performed" (5:6). As we have seen, this idiomatic expression means Esther can have anything she wants. You would think this carte blanche put in her hand would encourage her to say what is on her heart. But she is still anxious. Esther's anxiety is only more evidence that the Jews are far from God; yet God by His providence is overruling. So notice how gingerly she moves.

"Then answered Esther, and said, My petition and my request is; If I have found favour in the sight of the king, and if it please the king to grant my petition, and to perform my request, let the king and Haman come to the banquet that I shall prepare for them, and I will do to-morrow as the king hath said" (5:7,8). Esther does not have the courage yet to express her request, so she says, "I'm making another banquet tomorrow. We have had only a smorgasbord today, but come back tomorrow and I'll prepare a real banquet. Then I'll let you know my request." You can see the fear that is in the heart of this girl.

"Then went Haman forth that day joyful and with a

glad heart. . ." We really get acquainted with Haman now. ". . . but when Haman saw Mordecai in the king's gate, that he stood not up, nor moved for him, he was full of indignation against Mordecai" (5:9). This man Haman comes out from the banquet pleased with himself that only *he* has been the guest of the king and queen (you'll hear him brag in a moment). His ego has been greatly expanded. As he leaves the palace all the functionaries of the kingdom are there, and they all bow before him—except one, Mordecai the judge, who stands erect. You would think that a man in the position of Haman would ignore a little thing like that, but he is not ignoring anything. He is full of indignation against Mordecai and only restrains himself by thinking, *Well, I'll get even with you in a few days!*

". . . and when he came home, he sent and called for his friends, and Zeresh his wife" (5:10). Listen to Haman. "And Haman told them of the glory of his riches, and the multitude of his children . . ." (5:11). (Have you ever noticed that when a man starts bragging, he will tell you how much money he has made and about what fine children he has? Those are the two things a man of the world will brag about. And here was the man of the world, Haman.) ". . . and all the things wherein the king had promoted him, and how he had advanced him above the princes and servants of the king. Haman said moreover, Yea, Esther the queen did let no man come in with the king unto the banquet that she had prepared but myself; and tomorrow am I invited unto her also with the king" (5:11,12).

Listen to him brag! There is a Greek proverb that says, "Whom the gods would destroy they first make mad." This was the position of Haman exactly. Or, as the Scriptures put it, "Pride goeth before destruction, and an haughty spirit before a fall" (Prov. 16:18).

This fellow Haman, walking up and down bragging, calling in his friends, telling them how rich he is, telling about his children, then telling about the important position he holds—does he sound like anyone you know? Unfortunately, sometimes you hear Christians bragging like this, and they ought not.

Haman boasts, "And just think of it—I had lunch today with the queen, and not only that, I'm having dinner there tomorrow night." Well, he doesn't know what is in store for him. He would do well to turn down *that* invitation, but not this man.

There is, however, a fly in the ointment. He adds, "Yet all this availeth me nothing, so long as I see Mordecai the Jew sitting at the king's gate" (5:13). *"He won't bow to me!"* Someone has said that you can always tell the size of a man by the things that irritate him. If little things irritate him, he is a little man. If it takes big things to irritate him, he is a big man.

My friend, what bothers you? Do little things annoy you? In the church today how many people say, "Mrs. Jones didn't speak to me today" or "I was at the morning service and the minister looked right at me, but later he did not shake my hand; I feel so miserable about it." Don't let insignificant things mar your life. That is the mark of littleness. Yet most of us must confess that it is the small things, the "little foxes that spoil the vines" as far as our own lives are concerned.

Haman revealed himself to be a little man. After all, Mordecai was only a judge, a petty judge, in the kingdom. Haman was prime minister. He could have ignored the fellow! But not Haman. "All this availeth me nothing, so long as I see Mordecai the Jew sitting at the king's gate" (5:13).

Haman's "lovely" wife offered a solution. "Then said Zeresh his wife and all his friends unto him, Let a gallows be made of fifty cubits high, and to-morrow speak thou unto the king that Mordecai may be hanged thereon: then go thou in merrily with the king unto the banquet. And the thing pleased Haman; and he caused the gallows to be made" (5:14).

Late that evening workmen constructed a gallows fifty cubits high (that's about seventy-five feet). Think of that! Consider it in light of the meaning of the name *Mordecai*. It means "little man"—Mordecai was a short fellow. To erect a gallows seventy-five feet high on which to hang a short fellow reveals the extent of the resentment, the hatred, and the bitterness in Haman's heart. So with his happy solution he went to bed.

Night came, which brings us to the most fateful night, the most eventful night in the history of the Medo-Persian Empire, the night which is the turning point of the Book of Esther. That night the king could not sleep. It was a little thing, you may say, a trivial incident. Most of us have missed a night's sleep at one time or another.

Have you noticed that God uses the little things to carry out His program? At one time God brought together a woman's heart and a baby's cry to change the destiny of a people. That baby's cry was what drew Pharaoh's daughter to the water's edge. As she looked down into the puckered face of the baby alone in the basket, her woman's heart went out to him. She took Moses and reared him as her own. God used a baby's cry.

Coming to the New Testament, we find examples of God's use of little things. On Easter we talk at length about the tomb being sealed and the stone rolled away, but do you know the greatest proof of the resurrection of Jesus Christ? It was the evidence that convinced Peter and John. They saw the linen wrappings lying flat. The body of Jesus had been prepared for burial like a mummy, wrapped around and around with a linen cloth and sealed with myrrh. The apostles knew Jesus could not get out unless He was unwound, but He was out—and there remained the grave clothes, still wound. They saw and they believed! God used the simple medium of grave clothes to prove the resurrection of Jesus.

A supposedly unimportant situation developed at the palace of Shushan: the king could not sleep. "On that night could not the king sleep, and he commanded to bring the book of records of the chronicles; and they were read before the king" (6:1). This proved to be an epochal night in that kingdom; the fatal hour had come, and the hand of God was moving. The king had insomnia, I suspect. After all, in his position the sword of Damocles was over his head all the time. As it has been said, "Uneasy lies the head that wears the crown" as well as "A good conscience is a luxury that only a righteous man can enjoy."

Ahasuerus, we happen to know from secular history, was not a righteous man. When he couldn't sleep that night, he wasn't able to call for an array of sleeping pills or tranquilizers like we have today, but he did have something to induce sleep which apparently he had used before. It was the book of records of the chronicles, that is, the detailed records of the kingdom. A servant was summoned to drone off this record, which was like a log or the minutes of the kingdom.

I do not mean to be unlovely, but to me the most boring thing in the world is to listen to minutes. Have you ever heard any minutes that were interesting? I never have. I've been on mission boards, I've been on church boards, I've been on all kinds of boards, and I've gotten off every board I can get off. You know why? I don't like to listen to minutes. They're boring. I can understand that this king went to sleep many a night with them being read to him. "Bring them in. Let's read them again."

On that particular night the reader happened to turn. . . . Did I say "happened" to turn? Yes, from his viewpoint. If you had been there with this servant and said, "Do you know that you turned to the right page?" he would have answered, "I don't know anything about that. I just opened the book, and I'm going to begin reading right here." But the hand of God was moving, because what he read began a chain of reactions that changed the course of history. Here it is: "And it was found written, that Mordecai had told of Bigthana and Teresh, two of the king's chamberlains, the keepers of the door, who sought to lay hand on the king Ahasuerus" (6:2).

Talk about the Mafia—these two fellows had belonged to the Mafia of that day. Mordecai had overheard them plotting, the kind of plotting that we always think of in connection with the Persian Empire: shadowy figures behind pillars, talking in low tones of how, when the king comes in, they'll put a dagger in him. Mordecai had passed that word on to Queen Esther, and Queen Esther had notified the king. The incident was entered in the records of the kingdom. When the chamberlain read this, the king was alerted, and he rose up in bed. He said, "By the way, you didn't read there—or I must have missed it—was this man Mordecai rewarded?" The servant looked down, read the next set of minutes, and said, "No, he was never rewarded." The king said, "The man who saved my life must be rewarded!"

At that moment there is a noise outside the king's chambers—a gate opening and closing, and some-one coming in. "And the king said, Who is in the court? . . ." Somebody else can not sleep this night. ". . . Now Haman was come into the outer court of the king's house, to speak unto the king to hang Mordecai on the gallows that he had prepared for him" (6:4). Haman's appearance is no accident. The providence of God is moving in that kingdom as the providence of God moves in the lives and hearts of many today.

One evening a young man attended a service where I was preaching. He held the doubtful distinction of being a most successful gambler at the Las Vegas casi-nos. His wife had left him and had taken the children with her. He did not know where they were, and it was breaking his heart. On this particular evening he had come to our city and was eating at a restaurant where one of our church members was having dinner. Seeing this young man and sensing that he was in deep sorrow of some nature, she ventured over and quietly sat down beside him. During the conversation she extended an invitation to our evening worship. He accepted and sat at the rear of the church. At the close of the service when we asked those who wished to accept Christ to come forward, he was one of the

number who came. He had come to the church that
night by the providence of God, and the sceptre of
grace was extended to him.

Out of the long ago comes this story of Esther. It
speaks to our twentieth century of the sceptre of grace
that is extended to a lost world. People today are
sinners; people today deserve the judgment of God;
people today are dead in trespasses and sins. But
people today can come to God on one basis alone, by
receiving Christ who said, ". . . I am the way, the
truth, and the life: no man cometh unto the Father, but
by me" (John 14:6).

# ·7·

## The Man Who Came to Dinner but Died on the Gallows

*Esther, Chapters 6:4–7:10*

And the king said, Who is in the court? Now Haman was come into the outward court of the king's house, to speak unto the king to hang Mordecai on the gallows that he had prepared for him. And the king's servants said unto him, Behold, Haman standeth in the court. And the king said, Let him come in. So Haman came in. And the king said unto him, What shall be done unto the man whom the king delighteth to honour? Now Haman thought in his heart, To whom would the king delight to do honour more than to myself? And Haman answered the king, For the man whom the king delighteth to honour, let the royal apparel be brought which the king useth to wear, and the horse that the king rideth upon, and the crown royal which is set upon his head: and let this apparel and horse be delivered to the hand of one of the king's most noble princes, that they may array the man withal whom the king delighteth to honour, and bring him on horseback

through the street of the city, and proclaim before
him, Thus shall it be done to the man whom the
king delighteth to honour. Then the king said to
Haman, Make haste, and take the apparel and the
horse, as thou hast said, and do even so to Mordecai the Jew, that sitteth at the king's gate: let
nothing fail of all that thou hast spoken. Then
took Haman the apparel and the horse, and
arrayed Mordecai, and brought him on horseback
through the street of the city, and proclaimed
before him, Thus shall it be done unto the man
whom the king delighteth to honour.

And Mordecai came again to the king's gate.
But Haman hastened to his house mourning, and
having his head covered. And Haman told Zeresh
his wife and all his friends every thing that had
befallen him. Then said his wise men and Zeresh
his wife unto him, If Mordecai be of the seed of
the Jews, before whom thou hast begun to fall,
thou shalt not prevail against him, but shalt surely
fall before him. And while they were yet talking
with him, came the king's chamberlains, and
hasted to bring Haman unto the banquet that
Esther had prepared.

So the king and Haman came to banquet with
Esther the queen. And the king said again unto
Esther on the second day at the banquet of wine,
What is thy petition, queen Esther? and it shall be
granted thee: and what is thy request? and it shall
be performed, even to the half of the kingdom.
Then Esther the queen answered and said, If I
have found favour in thy sight, O king, and if it
please the king, let my life be given me at my
petition, and my people at my request: For we are

sold, I and my people, to be destroyed, to be slain, and to perish. But if we had been sold for bondmen and bondwomen, I had held my tongue, although the enemy could not countervail the king's damage.

Then the king Ahasuerus answered and said unto Esther the queen, Who is he, and where is he, that durst presume in his heart to do so? And Esther said, The adversary and enemy is this wicked Haman. Then Haman was afraid before the king and the queen.

And the king arising from the banquet of wine in his wrath went into the palace garden: and Haman stood up to make request for his life to Esther the queen; for he saw that there was evil determined against him by the king. Then the king returned out of the palace garden into the place of the banquet of wine; and Haman was fallen upon the bed whereon Esther was. Then said the king, Will he force the queen also before me in the house? As the word went out of the king's mouth, they covered Haman's face. And Harbonah, one of the chamberlains, said before the king, Behold also, the gallows fifty cubits high, which Haman had made for Mordecai, who had spoken good for the king, standeth in the house of Haman. Then the king said, Hang him thereon. So they hanged Haman on the gallows that he had prepared for Mordecai. Then was the king's wrath pacified.

Early morning had come to the palace at Shushan, but sleep had not come to the king. There was another man also who had not slept that night, but for a different reason. You will recall that the king had been listening to the chronicles of his kingdom being read, hoping it would put him to sleep. But the servant had turned to the section that recorded the service Mordecai had performed in discovering the plot to put the king to death. The king, who was probably half asleep until he heard this, asked, ". . . What honour and dignity hath been done to Mordecai for this? Then said the king's servants that ministered unto him, There is nothing done for him" (6:3).

At that moment Haman is heard coming into the outer court. The king wants to know who has come so early. "And the king said, Who is in the court? Now Haman was come into the outward court of the king's house, to speak unto the king to hang Mordecai on the gallows that he had prepared for him" (6:4). The king is informed that it is Haman, and Haman comes in. Apparently he has entrée to the king at any time. When he comes in, the king brings him into the conversation without giving him any background. Haman has come to ask for the life of Mordecai at the same moment the king is preparing to reward Mordecai!

These circumstances continue to reveal the providence of God. In the shadows God is keeping watch over His own. Although these people were out of the will of God, in the land far away from where God wanted them, they were still not out from under His direct leading. These providential dealings could not have been accidental.

When Haman walks in he is greeted with the question, ". . . What shall be done unto the man whom the king delighteth to honour? Now Haman thought in his heart, To whom would the king delight to do honour more than to myself?" (6:6). After all, Haman has been made prime minister. He has been given the ring of the king. He has paid the king a handsome sum of money in order to exterminate the Jewish people, *in toto*. Certainly, there is no one else in the kingdom that Haman can think of that the king would delight to honor.

The true nature of this man is revealed in his answer. "And Haman answered the king, For the man whom the king delighteth to honour, let the royal apparel be brought which the king useth to wear, and the horse that the king rideth upon, and the crown royal which is set upon his head: and let this apparel and horse be delivered to the hand of one of the king's most noble princes, that they may array the man withal whom the king delighteth to honour, and bring him on horseback through the street of the city, and proclaim before him, Thus shall it be done to the man whom the king delighteth to honour" (6:7–9). I am sure you can see what is in the heart of Haman. Haman has his eye upon the throne. It is his intention, when the time is right, to eliminate the king; he wants to destroy him.

That was the story of the Persian monarchs, anyway. It was difficult for a man to stay on the throne very long. In Israel's history, as recorded in First and Second Kings, if it were not tragic it would be humorous to see how short a time some of the kings ruled. Some of them only made it through two months. If a king reigned as long as ten years in the northern kingdom, he was doing well. And when the king sat on his throne and looked around him, he didn't know who was his friend and who was his enemy. He realized that any man who was lifted up would attempt to slay him in order that he might become king.

Obviously such designs were in the heart of Haman. He was thinking, *To whom would the king delight to do honor more than to myself? You let me have the apparel of the king, put the crown on my head, let me ride the king's horse, let it be announced by a herald when I go through the streets.* What was Haman doing? He was preparing the people for the day when the crown and the royal apparel would be his. Surely Ahasuerus suspected this type of scheming, for he recognized that this man was thinking of himself and certainly not of Mordecai.

"Then the king said to Haman, Make haste, and take the apparel and the horse, as thou hast said, and do even so to Mordecai the Jew, that sitteth at the king's gate: let nothing fail of all that thou hast spoken" (6:10). For Haman, the decree was mortification beyond words. "Then took Haman the apparel and the horse, and arrayed Mordecai, and brought him on horseback through the street of the city, and proclaimed before him, Thus shall it be done unto the man whom the king delighteth to honour" (6:11). The humiliation of Haman was absolutely unspeakable. You can imagine the feeling that he had as he led the horse through the street with Mordecai—the man who wouldn't bow to him—seated on it, when Haman had at home a gallows seventy-five feet high on which to hang him!

Finally the ordeal was over. "And Mordecai came again to the king's gate. But Haman hastened to his house mourning, and having his head covered" (6:12). Shame beyond shame. "And Haman told Zeresh his wife and all his friends every thing that had befallen him. Then said his wise men and Zeresh his wife unto him, If Mordecai be of the seed of the Jews, before whom thou hast begun to fall, thou shalt not prevail against him, but shalt surely fall before him" (6:13). What comforting friends to have around, and how nice to have a wife like this, who tells you that probably tomorrow will be your last day! "And while they were yet talking with him, came the king's chamberlains, and hasted to bring Haman unto the banquet that Esther had prepared" (6:14). Things began to happen thick and fast. This man Haman no sooner arrived home and explained to his wife and his wise men what had happened and they cautioned him, than there was a knock at the door. The king's servants told him to hurry. The banquet was ready that he had promised to attend. Haman had looked forward to this, you remember. He had boasted about the fact that he was the only one whom the queen had invited to attend her banquet with the king. As was said earlier, this is an illustration of the Proverb: "Pride goeth before destruction, and an haughty spirit before a fall" (Prov. 16:18).

Esther has, if I may use the expression, screwed up her courage, after the second day, to tell what is on her heart. She could not bring herself to do it earlier, but the time has come.

"So the king and Haman came to banquet with Esther the queen. And the king said again unto Esther on the second day at the banquet of wine, What is thy petition, queen Esther? and it shall be granted thee: and what is thy request? and it shall be performed, even to the half of the kingdom" (7:1,2). For the third time Ahasuerus says to his lovely queen, "You may

ask what's on your mind. Tell me because I will grant
your request."

Now she is going to speak. It is a frightful thing that
Esther reveals, and there are two startled men there
that day because neither knows her nationality. As
you remember, when Mordecai, her cousin, entered
her in the beauty contest, and also when she became
queen, he instructed her not to tell her nationality.
Esther kept this fact to herself all this time. When
Haman sent out the edict that all the Jews in the
kingdom are to be destroyed, he had no idea that the
queen was a Jewess.

"Then Esther the queen answered and said, If I have
found favour in thy sight, O king, and if it please the
king, let my life be given me at my petition, and my
people at my request" (7:3). Esther finally identifies
herself with her people. Once so far removed from
God that she did not even want to be known as a
Jewess, she finally takes her place with her people. For
her to do so is to identify herself with her religion and
with her God.

Her plea is eloquent. "For we are sold, I and my
people, to be destroyed, to be slain, and to perish . . ."
(7:4). Those are the exact words used in the proclama-
tion that went out over the king's signature. " . . . But
if we had been sold for bondmen and bondwomen, I
had held my tongue, although the enemy could not
countervail the king's damage" (7:4). In other words,
Esther is saying, "Although the king would have suffered a great loss, I would have kept quiet if we were
just going to be sold into slavery. But that isn't the
case. We are to be *slain* on a certain day."

"Then the king Ahasuerus answered and said unto

Esther the queen, Who is he, and where is he, that durst presume in his heart to do so?" (7:5). Ahasuerus is startled. He is amazed. He does not dream that there is any such thing as that taking place in his kingdom. He apparently does not recognize even yet the people who are to be slain.

This only reiterated what little regard this man had for life. If you read the secular account of Xerxes' campaign which he made into Europe against Greece, you will find that he threw men about as if they all were expendable. He lost thousands and thousands of men in that campaign, but he was not disturbed one bit. Human life was very cheap in that day.

What disturbs Ahasuerus is that they are the people of Esther and that his queen is in mortal danger. He truly is asking a question, for he does not know "Who is he, and where is he, who would presume in his heart to do so?"

Remember that the man is Haman, who is there at the table, reclining on a couch. He is the prime minister, and he had the full confidence of the king. A similar situation would be going to the President of the United States to accuse the Secretary of State of some great crime against the President's wife.

Ahasuerus asks who the man is, and Esther reveals her bravery to the fullest. She is putting her life on the line by speaking the truth. "And Esther said, The adversary and enemy is this wicked Haman. Then Haman was afraid before the king and the queen" (7:6). Haman himself had not realized the extent of the decree that he has obtained against the Jews. He knew it included Mordecai, but he did not realize that it included Queen Esther! He is startled.

The king is so shocked at what he has heard that he cannot speak. "And the king arising from the banquet of wine in his wrath went into the palace garden . . ." (7:7). The sudden turn of events is so puzzling his head is swimming, and he has to go out and think his way through the sequence of events. *How in the world has it happened that a decree has gone out over my signature to slay my own queen?* he must have thought. *How could a thing like this happen in my kingdom?* After all, Ahasuerus is ultimately responsible for that decree. And so he goes out to think the matter over.

Haman is in a bad spot. ". . . and Haman stood up to make request for his life to Esther the queen; for he saw that there was evil determined against him by the king" (7:7). He begins to plead with Queen Esther, for he knows she is his only hope.

Haman, when he hears her accusation, leaps to his feet and begins pleading for his life. Seeing that he is getting nowhere, he grovels at her feet, then pulls himself up on her couch (you recall that the custom was to recline on couches while dining).

As we have noted, it is interesting that Herodotus, the Greek historian, recorded that when Xerxes returned after his defeat in the Greek campaign, the new queen whom he married was very vindictive and cold. If he was referring to Queen Esther it would be understandable that to the outside world and to the historian she would appear vindictive and cold in this situation. Haman was punished justly—but fearfully—for the thing that he had done.

"Then the king returned out of the palace garden into the place of the banquet of wine; and Haman was fallen upon the couch whereon Esther was . . ." (7:8).

Haman, coward that he is, is clawing in terror at her couch. The man is beside himself with fear. When the king comes in and sees the high sort of indignity that is taking place, he says, "Will he force the queen also before me in the house?"

This man's fate is sealed when the king sees that spectacle. " . . . As the word went out of the king's mouth, they covered Haman's face" (7:8).

Notice that Ahasuerus did not have to issue an order at all. He simply walked in, saw what was taking place, made the statement, and the servants who were standing there knew what to do. They took Haman out. Not only was he placed under palace guard and under house arrest, but he was executed that night— because the king happened to be the "Supreme Court" also. "And Harbonah, one of the chamberlains, said before the king, Behold also, the gallows fifty cubits high, which Haman had made for Mordecai, who had spoken good for the king, standeth in the house of Haman. Then the king said, Hang him thereon. So they hanged Haman on the gallows that he had prepared for Mordecai. Then was the king's wrath pacified" (7:9,10).

This is a revelation of a great truth that runs all the way through the Word of God. Paul annunciated it for believers, "Be not deceived; God is not mocked: for whatsoever a man soweth, that shall he also reap" (Gal. 6:7). Is it not interesting that the very gallows that Haman had prepared to hang an innocent man on was the gallows on which he was hanged?

You remember that Ahab was told by Elijah the prophet that right where the dogs licked the blood of Naboth, whom he brutally and cruelly murdered, there the dogs would lick his blood (see 1 Kin. 21:19). Ahab thought, *Well, I'll stay away from that place!* And he did. But after he was mortally wounded in battle, that is where his chariot was brought. The record says that one washed his chariot and his armor in the pool of Samaria and the dogs licked up his blood (see 1 Kin. 22:38).

Jacob experienced similar retribution. He deceived his father (see Gen. 27:1–29). Oh, he was a clever boy. He put on Esau's clothes; old Isaac smelled them and said, "It smells just like my son Esau." They had no lovely deodorants in that day, so when Esau came in, even if you didn't hear him, your other senses told you he had arrived. Jacob put goatskin on his hands, and blind old Isaac reached out and said, "It feels like Esau." Jacob thought he was clever. He was God's man, but God did not let him get by with sin. Years later, when he was old and the father of twelve sons, they brought to him the coat of many colors dipped in the blood of a goat (see Gen. 37:31–35). They said, "Is this your son's coat?" Old Jacob broke down and wept. He in turn was deceived about his favorite son.

This is an inexorable law of God. I believe it operates today as it has always operated, and it will operate in any field. Whatsoever a person sows, he'll reap. When you sow cotton, you reap cotton. When you sow corn, you reap corn. "For he that soweth to his flesh shall of the flesh reap corruption; but he that soweth to the Spirit shall of the Spirit reap life everlasting" (Gal. 6:8).

Paul knew a great deal about the operation of this law in his own experience. He was the man who apparently gave the orders for the stoning of Stephen (see Acts 7:57–8:1). They put their clothes at his feet, which indicates that he was in charge. But Paul didn't get by with it. You may say, "Well, he was converted. He came to Christ and his sins were forgiven." Yes, they were forgiven, but chickens always come home to roost. Whatever a man sows will be harvested. And Paul's seed did come up. On his first missionary journey he went into the Galatian country and came to Lystra, where the people stoned him and left him for dead (see Acts 14:19,20). I believe he *was* dead, and that's the reason they left him. God raised him from the dead, but Paul experienced the truth of these words: "Whatsoever a man soweth, that shall he also reap." God is not mocked.

Haman experienced the same thing. He learned this law the hard way. Here was a man who went to dinner and found out it was a necktie party. They hanged him!

May I call your attention to two Scriptures as we conclude this chapter. The first passage is a general statement.

I have seen the wicked in great power, and spreading himself like a green bay tree. Yet he passed away, and, lo, he was not: yea, I sought him, but he could not be found (Ps. 37:35,36).

Do you remember Adolph Hitler? I heard a Presbyterian preacher in Texas years ago say, even when Hitler was going great guns, "When the time comes, God will stop him." He did. It's interesting: Mussolini, Stalin—consider any one of them—"Yet he passed away, and lo, he was not: yea, I sought him, but he could not be found."

Now the second verse of Scripture is one of the

greatest statements in the Word of God concerning the nation Israel. It is found in Isaiah's prophecy.

> No weapon that is formed against thee shall prosper; and every tongue that shall rise against thee in judgment thou shalt condemn. This is the heritage of the servants of the LORD, and their righteousness is of me, saith the LORD (Is. 54:17).

That is a tremendous statement!

Haman died on that cursed gallows because there was no one to die for him. Let us go forward in history for a moment, when there was another man in prison. His name was Barabbas, and he was condemned to die. They already had made a cross for him to die on. He waited that long night through, knowing the next morning he was to be crucified. In the morning he heard the jailer coming, and he heard the clank of the keys. He heard him turn the key in his cell door and that old door creak open. He mustered his courage, for he knew his time had come. The jailer came in and said to Barabbas, "You are free!"

"What do you mean 'You're free'?" Barabbas asked. "What are you trying to do—amuse yourself with me? Ridicule me? I'm to die."

"No, you're not to die."

"Well, why am I not to die?"

"Because last night a Man was arrested, and this morning they found Him guilty. Pilate wanted to let Him go. He offered to release Him, and he gave the people a choice: 'Jesus or Barabbas?' The crowd said, 'Release Barabbas.' Jesus is going to die on your cross, Barabbas." I do not know this, but I assume this is how it was.

Although the record does not say, I think Barabbas went out to Calvary that day, looked up, and said, "That's my cross. That is where I deserve to die." And I like to think that he found out, as the centurion found and as the thief found that the One dying there did not deserve to die (see Luke 23:39–47). Not only that, but He was dying for another. He was the Son of man who ". . . came not to be ministered unto, but to minister, and to give His life a ransom for many" (Matt. 20:28). At least Barabbas knew that Somebody else died for him. Haman had no one to die for him.

You and I stand guilty before God as sinners. We deserve exactly the condemnation of Haman. You may say, "I never committed a crime like that." Who said you did? But you have the same kind of human nature that he had, which is in rebellion against God and which is opposed to God. In that state, while you were dead in trespasses and sins, Christ died for you and took your place on the cross. That cross not only was Barabbas' cross, it was my cross, and it was your cross, if you'll have it that way and will trust Him. He died in our stead.

# · 8 ·

## *The Message of Hope That Went Out From the King*

*Esther, Chapter 8*

On that day did the king Ahasuerus give the house of Haman the Jews' enemy unto Esther the queen. And Mordecai came before the king; for Esther had told what he was unto her. And the king took off his ring, which he had taken from Haman, and gave it unto Mordecai. And Esther set Mordecai over the house of Haman.

And Esther spake yet again before the king, and fell down at his feet, and besought him with tears to put away the mischief of Haman the Agagite, and his device that he had devised against the Jews. Then the king held out the golden sceptre toward Esther. So Esther arose, and stood before the king, and said, If it please the king, and if I have found favour in his sight, and the thing seem right before the king, and I be pleasing in his eyes, let it be written to reverse the letters devised by Haman the son of Hammedatha the Agagite, which he wrote to destroy the Jews which are in all the king's provinces: for how can I endure to see the evil that shall come unto my people? or how can I endure to see the destruction of my kindred?

Then the king Ahasuerus said unto Esther the queen and to Mordecai the Jew, Behold, I have given Esther the house of Haman, and him they have hanged upon the gallows, because he laid his hand upon the Jews. Write ye also for the Jews, as it liketh you, in the king's name, and seal it with the king's ring: for the writing which is written in the king's name, and sealed with the king's ring, may no man reverse. Then were the king's scribes called at that time in the third month, that is, the month Sivan, on the three and twentieth day thereof; and it was written according to all that Mordecai commanded unto the Jews, and to the lieutenants, and the deputies and rulers of the provinces which are from India unto Ethiopia, an hundred twenty and seven provinces, unto every province according to the writing thereof, and unto every people after their language, and to the Jews according to their writing, and according to their language. And he wrote in the king Ahasuerus' name, and sealed it with the king's ring, and sent letters by posts on horseback, and riders on mules, camels, and young dromedaries: wherein the king granted the Jews which were in every city to gather themselves together, and to stand for their life, to destroy, to slay, and to cause to perish, all the power of the people and province that would assault them, both little ones and women, and to take the spoil of them for a prey, upon one day in all the provinces of king Ahasuerus, namely, upon the

thirteenth day of the twelfth month, which is the
month Adar. The copy of the writing for a commandment to be given in every province was published unto all people, and that the Jews should be
ready against that day to avenge themselves on
their enemies. So the posts that rode upon mules
and camels went out, being hastened and pressed
on by the king's commandment. And the decree
was given at Shushan the palace.

And Mordecai went out from the presence of
the king in royal apparel of blue and white, and
with a great crown of gold, and with a garment of
fine linen and purple: and the city of Shushan
rejoiced and was glad. The Jews had light, and
gladness, and joy, and honour. And in every
province, and in every city, whithersoever the
king's commandment and his decree came, the
Jews had joy and gladness, a feast and a good day.
And many of the people of the land became Jews;
for the fear of the Jews fell upon them.

Our study closed in the previous chapter with the
judgment pronounced upon Haman and the execution
of that judgment. Additionally, Queen Esther was
given power over all of Haman's household, who
might do her or her people harm. That, however, did
not alter the decree that had gone out against the Jews.
The decree still stood: On a certain day the Jews in the
127 provinces, all the way from India to Ethiopia, were
to be destroyed. This included even the remnant who
had returned to the Promised Land. That small remnant was struggling to rebuild the walls, the city, and
the temple in Jerusalem; no doubt their enemies were
awaiting eagerly the day when the decree would be

effective. There was to be a great slaughter: the destruction of the Jews throughout the empire.

". . . And Mordecai came before the king; for Esther had told what he was unto her. And the king took off his ring, which he had taken from Haman, and gave it unto Mordecai. And Esther set Mordecai over the house of Haman" (8:1,2). For the first time Esther let it be known that Mordecai was her adoptive father—Mordecai, the man whose refusal to bow to Haman had occasioned this terrible decree.

Evidently Ahasuerus was quite free with the use of his ring. It was a powerful and important ring. It could be pressed down into wax to seal a law that would destroy people. The ring passed on to Mordecai was the ring Ahasuerus had entrusted to Haman when Haman was prime minister. The ring came to be in good hands, but it tells us something about Ahasuerus, that he was very careless in passing his power around.

"And Esther spake yet again before the king, and fell down at his feet, and besought him with tears to put away the mischief of Haman the Agagite, and his device that he had devised against the Jews" (8:3). When Queen Esther realized for the first time that Haman's decree could not be altered, she made a plea for her people and cried for help. But the solution wasn't as simple as she had thought. The king could not sit down and cancel the previous order.

It was impossible to change the decree. Even the king could not change it. According to the law of the Medes and the Persians, Ahasuerus must bow to his own law. We had seen this already in reference to his first queen, Vashti. When he made the decree to set her aside, then later wanted to take her back, the decree said he could not. Even the king could not break his own decree, and he was powerless to change the decree concerning the destruction of the Jews.

So Queen Esther tried a different strategy. She came into the king's presence, and he was gracious once again and extended to her his golden sceptre. Then Esther said, "If it please the king, and if I have found favour in his sight, and the thing seem right before the king, and I be pleasing in his eyes, let it be written to reverse the letters devised by Haman the son of Hammedatha the Agagite, which he wrote to destroy the Jews which are in all the king's provinces: For how can I endure to see the evil that shall come unto my people? or how can I endure to see the destruction of my kindred?" (8:5,6).

Esther made it quite plain to the king that the judgment against Haman was of no avail unless her people were rescued as well. Something had to be done to save them.

"Then the king Ahasuerus said unto Esther the queen and to Mordecai the Jew, Behold, I have given Esther the house of Haman, and him they have hanged upon the gallows, because he laid his hand upon the Jews" (8:7). The king had given to Esther and to Mordecai the house of Haman, but that was still no solution to the decree of death.

Finally Ahasuerus shrugged his shoulders and said, "Write ye also for the Jews, as it liketh you, in the king's name, and seal it with the king's ring: for the writing which is written in the king's name, and sealed with the king's ring, may no man reverse" (8:8).

With that, Mordecai went into action. He could not revoke the day of slaughter for his people, but he could send out a new order, and the new order permitted the Jews to defend themselves. Under the first order, the Jews could no more have defended themselves than they could have in Hitler's gas chambers. They would have been slaughtered like animals. But under the new decree they were permitted to defend themselves.

Additionally, the government declared their support of the Jews. We read, "And all the rulers of the provinces, and the lieutenants, and the deputies, and officers of the king, helped the Jews; because the fear of Mordecai fell upon them" (9:3). The entire power of the king, as evidenced by his army and his officers, aligned themselves on the side of the Jews. That changed the entire picture. When this new decree came to the different provinces, we're told "The Jews had light, and gladness, and joy, and honour" (8:16). The first decree also had brought sadness to a great many people other than the Jews, as was the case in Nazi Germany. There were a great many German people who were saddened by the gas chambers and embarrassed by them. Many have shown evidences of real repentance since then; but at the time they could do little in the face of Hitler's decrees. Nothing was done for the Jew at that time; neither could anything be done in the time of Esther until this new decree was made.

As we read this record, we can imagine the sequence of events. It must have been late in the evening that Queen Esther went again into the presence of the king to plead for her people. Then the new decree was written and was signed with the king's ring. "Mordecai went out from the presence of the king in royal apparel of blue and white, and with a great crown of gold, and with a garment of fine linen and purple:

and the city of Shushan rejoiced and was glad" (8:15).

The royal apparel Mordecai donned certainly was different from the sackcloth and ashes he had worn only a short time earlier. His appearance in the city undoubtedly reinforced the joy produced by the king's new decree. Notice the contrast between the two decrees: Haman's decree produced sorrow, but Mordecai's decree produced joy.

Persia was a polyglot kingdom—many languages were spoken. To spread the word, amanuenses had to be summoned to write the decree in the languages of the 127 provinces, and probably there were hundreds of copies for each language.

"And he wrote in the king Ahasuerus' name, and sealed it with the king's ring, and sent letters by posts on horseback, and riders on mules, camels, and young dromedaries: Wherein the king granted the Jews which were in every city to gather themselves together, and to stand for their life, to destroy, to slay, and to cause to perish, all the power of the people and province that would assault them, both little ones and women, and to take the spoil of them for a prey,

"Upon one day in all the provinces of king Ahasuerus, namely, upon the thirteenth day of the twelfth month, which is the month Adar" (8:10–12).

The kingdom employed all the means of communication common to that day. Haste was of the essence. If the Jews heard the new decree—and believed it—they would be saved. Heralds were sent on horseback, on mules, on camels, and on dromedaries—across the Arabian Desert, up the Euphrates and Tigris rivers, down into India, and even into Africa. The heralds were riding in every direction, getting the decree out as quickly as possible to every village and hamlet in the kingdom. Because the original decree could not be altered in any way, another decree was made and sent out just as the first one was. It was signed by the king, and the entire power of the king was now on the side of the Jews.

One can picture easily the scene in any one of these little towns. The Jews, garbed in sackcloth and ashes, were hopeless and full of despair. They had been marked out and kept under the constant derision of their enemies, who doubtless were reminding them of the approaching day of their destruction. But then a rider appeared on the horizon, the first to arrive since the carrier who had born the decree of destruction. Quickly this rider approached the town bulletin board and nailed a notice there, then just as quickly mounted his steed again and was off. Everybody crowded around the bulletin board to see what was written. They read that the tables had been turned; the king was on the side of those people who formerly had been marked for death. He even urged them to band together and protect themselves. The Jews began to move gingerly into the crowd, hesitant because the last time they had gone to the bulletin board they were confronted with the terrible news that they were to be destroyed. Cautiously they came up; then as they began to read the message, they could not believe their eyes.

It was too glorious to be true! Something had happened, for now the king was on their side. They were to be spared, saved! What good news it was and what rejoicing there was among these people! The king was holding out the sceptre of grace to them. There was no longer judgment; there was grace.

# ·9·

## The Feast of Joy

*Esther, Chapters 9 and 10*

Now in the twelfth month, that is, the month
Adar, on the thirteenth day of the same, when the
king's commandment and his decree drew near to
be put in execution, in the day that the enemies of
the Jews hoped to have power over them, (though
it was turned to the contrary, that the Jews had
rule over them that hated them;) The Jews
gathered themselves together in their cities
throughout all the provinces of the king Ahasuerus, to lay hand on such as sought their hurt:
and no man could withstand them; for the fear of
them fell upon all people. And all the rulers of the
provinces, and the lieutenants, and the deputies,
and officers of the king, helped the Jews; because
the fear of Mordecai fell upon them. For Mordecai
was great in the king's house, and his fame went
out throughout all the provinces: for this man
Mordecai waxed greater and greater. Thus the
Jews smote all their enemies with the stroke of the

sword, and slaughter, and destruction, and did what they would unto those that hated them. And in Shushan the palace the Jews slew and destroyed five hundred men. And Parshandatha, and Dalphon, and Aspatha, and Poratha, and Adalia, and Aridatha, and Parmashta, and Arisai, and Aridai, and Vajezatha. The ten sons of Haman the son of Hammedatha, the enemy of the Jews, slew they; but on the spoil laid they not their hand. On that day the number of those that were slain in Shushan the palace was brought before the king.

And the king said unto Esther the queen, The Jews have slain and destroyed five hundred men in Shushan the palace, and the ten sons of Haman; what have they done in the rest of the king's provinces? now what is thy petition? and it shall be granted thee: or what is thy request further? and it shall be done. Then said Esther, If it please the king, let it be granted to the Jews which are in Shushan to do tomorrow also according unto this day's decree, and let Haman's ten sons be hanged upon the gallows. And the king commanded it so to be done: and the decree was given at Shushan; and they hanged Haman's ten sons. For the Jews that were in Shushan gathered themselves together on the fourteenth day also of the month Adar, and slew three hundred men at Shushan; but on the prey they laid not their hand. But the other Jews that were in the king's provinces gathered themselves together, and stood for their lives, and had rest from their enemies, and slew of their foes seventy and five thousand, but they laid not their hands on the prey, On the thirteenth day of the month Adar; and on the fourteenth day of the same rested they, and made it a day of feasting and gladness. But the Jews that were at Shushan assembled together on the thirteenth day thereof, and on the fourteenth thereof; and on the fifteenth day of the same they rested, and made it a day of feasting and gladness. Therefore the Jews of the villages that dwelt in the unwalled towns, made the fourteenth day of the month Adar a day of gladness and feasting, and a good day, and of sending portions one to another.

And Mordecai wrote these things, and sent letters unto all the Jews that were in all the provinces of the king Ahasuerus, both nigh and far, to stablish this among them, that they should keep the fourteenth day of the month Adar, and the fifteenth day of the same, yearly, as the days wherein the Jews rested from their enemies, and the month which was turned unto them from sorrow to joy, and from mourning into a good day: that they should make them days of feasting and joy, and of sending portions one to another, and gifts to the poor. And the Jews undertook to do as they had begun, and as Mordecai had written unto them; because Haman the son of Hammedatha, the Agagite, the enemy of all the Jews, had devised against the Jews to destroy them, and had cast Pur, that is, the lot, to consume them, and to destroy them; but when Esther came before the king, he commanded by letters that his wicked device, which he devised against the Jews, should return upon his own head, and that he and his sons should be hanged on the gallows. Wherefore they called these days Purim after the name of Pur. Therefore for all the words of this letter, and of that which they had seen concerning this matter, and which had come unto them, the Jews ordained, and took upon them, and upon their seed, and upon all such as joined themselves unto them, so as it should not fail, that they would keep these two days according to their writing, and according to their appointed time every year; and that these days should be remembered and kept throughout every generation, every family, every province, and every city; and that these days of Purim should not fail from among the Jews, nor the memorial of them perish from their seed. Then Esther the queen, the daughter of Abihail, and Mordecai the Jew, wrote with all authority, to confirm this second letter of Purim. And he sent the letters unto all the Jews, to the hundred twenty and seven provinces of the kingdom of Ahasuerus, with words of peace and truth, to confirm these days of Purim in their times appointed, according as Mordecai the Jew and Esther the queen had enjoined them, and as they had decreed for themselves and for their seed, the matters of the fastings and their cry. And the decree of Esther confirmed these matters of Purim; and it was written in the book.

And the king Ahasuerus laid a tribute upon the land, and upon the isles of the sea. And all the acts of his power and of his might, and the declaration of the greatness of Mordecai, whereunto the king advanced him, are they not written in the

book of the chronicles of the kings of Media and
Persia? For Mordecai the Jew was next unto king
Ahasuerus, and great among the Jews, and
accepted of the multitude of his brethren, seeking
the wealth of his people, and speaking peace to all
his seed.

As we see in the ninth chapter of the Book of Esther,
the anti-Semitic element still tried to carry out their
nefarious plan. I'm of the opinion that very few of the
Jews were slain. (Scripture gives no evidence that they
were.) Instead, "the Jews smote all their enemies with
the stroke of the sword, and slaughter, and destruction, and did what they would unto those that hated
them" (9:5).

There are people who feel that it was brutal and
cruel for a court of law to sentence many of Hitler's
henchmen to prison, but those henchmen were rascals
of the first order. Their treatment of the Jews in con-
centration camps was absolutely inhuman. To many
people on the outside it did not look as if Hitler's men
should be treated with such harshness, but those who
knew the inside story knew that they were rewarded
with justice.

"And all the rulers of the provinces, and the lieutenants, and the deputies, and officers of the king,
helped the Jews; because the fear of Mordecai fell
upon them. For Mordecai was great in the king's
house, and his fame went out throughout all the provinces: for this man Mordecai waxed greater and greater" (9:3,4).

For once Mordecai, one of their own, was by the
side of the king. Haman, who would have put the

Jews to death, had been put to death. The very throne that had once condemned the Jews protected them.

After this marvelous deliverance, a celebration was instituted called the Feast of Purim. "And Mordecai wrote these things, and sent letters unto all the Jews that were in all the provinces of the king Ahasuerus, both nigh and far, to stablish this among them, that they should keep the fourteenth day of the month Adar, and the fifteenth day of the same, yearly, as the days wherein the Jews rested from their enemies, and the month which was turned unto them from sorrow to joy, and from mourning into a good day: that they should make them days of feasting and joy, and of sending portions one to another, and gifts to the poor" (9:20–22).

The Jews still celebrate the Feast of Purim each year. (Adar is the month of March). *Purim* comes from the word *pur*, meaning "lots." Haman rolled the pur like dice to determine the day of the Jews' execution. "Because Haman the son of Hammedatha, the Agagite, the enemy of all the Jews, had devised against the Jews to destroy them, and had cast Pur, that is, the lot, to consume them, and to destroy them. . . . Wherefore they called these days Purim after the name of Pur. Therefore for all the words of this letter, and of that which they had seen concerning this matter, and which had come unto them, the Jews ordained, and took upon them, and upon their seed, and upon all such as joined themselves unto them, so as it should not fail, that they would keep these two days according to their writing, and according to their appointed time every year" (9:24–27).

(Incidentally, the unnamed feast mentioned in the

fifth chapter of the Gospel of John could not be the
Feast of Purim, as some hold, because the Jews were
not required to go to Jerusalem for Purim, and no
sacrifice was offered. Purim was celebrated throughout the empire of Persia.)

In our day the Feast of Purim still is commemorated
by the Jews. The day preceding is the "Fast of Esther."
On the first evening, the festival begins with a con-
vocation in their synagogues, concluded by the reading of the Book of Esther. As the Scriptures are read,
the listeners stamp on the floor whenever the name of
Haman is mentioned, saying, "Let his name be blotted
out. The name of the wicked will rot." And at the end
of the reading they say, "Cursed be Haman; blessed be
Mordecai!" Then the following morning they come to
the synagogue again. The remainder of the festival is a
time of rejoicing to celebrate the great fact that God has
delivered them (they also include subsequent deliver-
ances such as from the Nazi German atrocities) according to the promise that He made to Abraham. God
said, "I will bless them that bless thee, and curse him
that curseth thee . . ." (Gen. 12:3).

The Book of Esther concludes with this interesting
sidelight in chapter 10: "And the king Ahasuerus laid a
tribute upon the land, and upon the isles of the sea.
And all the acts of his power and of his might, and the
declaration of the greatness of Mordecai, whereunto
the king advanced him, are they not written in the
book of the chronicles of the kings of Media and Persia? For Mordecai the Jew was next unto king Ahasuerus, and great among the Jews, and accepted of the
multitude of his brethren, seeking the wealth of his
people, and speaking peace to all his seed (10:1–3).

Let us stop for a moment to think through the history of the world, noticing in particular the nations that have engaged in anti-Semitism and seeing where they are today. For example, consider the nations of Europe. During World War I people lamented the plight of "poor little Belgium." Do you want to know about poor little Belgium? It had instituted an awful siege of anti-Semitism. God says, "I will bless them that bless thee, and curse him that curseth thee." Look at Spain. Spain was the first nation to bring her flag into the Western Hemisphere. What happened to her greatness? Spain conducted the Inquisition. We think of the Spanish Inquisition as being against Protestants, but it was primarily against Jews. Spain lost her power. The Jews have attended the funeral of every nation that has attempted to destroy them. Babylon attempted it. Assyria attempted it. Egypt attempted it. And the glory of those nations lies in the dust. It would be well for our nation to take note of this fact.

In the end Ahasuerus celebrated the presence of the Jews in his own nation, and the Feast of Purim that the Jews celebrate each year sets forth that fact in a very vivid way.

As we conclude our study of the Book of Esther, let's draw a parallel. A decree has gone out from almighty God: "The soul that sinneth, it shall die . . ." (Ezek. 18:20). God has said also, "All have sinned, and come short of the glory of God" (Rom. 3:23). He says that the entire world stands before Him dead in trespasses and sins, waiting to be executed. He says that the world today is guilty and that the death penalty must prevail.

Now there are a great many softhearted and soft-headed liberal theologians who have taken the position that God forgives sin simply because He is bighearted, He has forgotten His law, He has changed it, or He has become a weakling. Liberalism in this century has depicted God as a senile old man sitting on a cloud. He has no notion of carrying through any kind of a decree that says, "The soul that sinneth, it shall die." You hear sloppy teaching about God being a God of "love." If the expression "God is dead" means that the liberal god is dead, then I'll attend his funeral. I'm glad he's dead. But the God of the Bible is quite different. God has not changed—not one whit. His decree about sin holds today one hundred percent. The idea that we are getting by with sin is a lie. We are getting by with nothing!

"Well," you may say, "it *looks* as if we are getting by with it." The psalmist thought so too. He wrote (in Psalm 73), "I was envious at the foolish, when I saw the prosperity of the wicked. For there are no bands in their death: but their strength is firm. They are not in trouble as other men; neither are they plagued like other men" (vv. 3–5). That disturbed him, and he wondered about it. Then he said: "When I thought to know this, it was too painful for me; until I went into the sanctuary of God; then understood I their end" (vv. 16,17). In other words, "In the temple I found out that God has a whole lot of time on His hands, and He doesn't have to move today or tomorrow, next week or even next month. He has eternity out yonder ahead of Him, and He moves according to His schedule. I found out that the wicked finally are judged, that God does deal with them."

I can remember (maybe you are old enough to remember, too) that when Hitler was going great guns, many people said, "Why doesn't God stop Hitler?" Where is Hitler today? God has plenty of time on His hands. He doesn't have to move today against the wicked, but His decree stands: "The soul that sinneth, it shall die."

However, this is not the end of the story. God has another decree that has gone out from heaven. That decree is: "For God so loved the world, that he gave his only begotten Son, that whosoever believeth in him should not perish . . ." because He bore the penalty (John 3:16). God cannot change His first decree, but He can send out another decree: a decree of grace that Another, His own Son, has paid the penalty for your sins and mine.

When God forgives today, He loves. Don't forget that He loves, but He loves in the context of the Cross. You do not find the love of God anywhere in this world but in the Cross of Christ.

You will not find God's love in nature. Within a block of my home, four teen-agers came careening down the street the other day, and their car, a little Volkswagen, went out of control. One of the passengers was killed; the others were rushed to the hospital. This world in which we live operates according to hard law. The law of gravity has not been repealed. None of God's laws have been repealed. But, thank God, the grace of God can reach down and save any sinner who will come in under the provision He has made. That is love.

That is good news. In fact, the literal meaning of the word *gospel* is "good news." The gospel, correctly in-

terpreted, is good news for the human family. The
gospel is defined for us by the apostle Paul in the
fifteenth chapter of First Corinthians: "Moreover,
brethren, I declare unto you the gospel which I
preached unto you, which also ye have received, and
wherein ye stand; by which also ye are saved . . ."
(vv. 1,2). The gospel is what saves men today. The
gospel is what Someone has done for us. The gospel is
not a request on God's part for you and me to do
something. On the contrary, the gospel is what He has
done for us. Here is what Paul says the gospel is: "For
I delivered unto you first of all that which I also received, how that Christ died for our sins according to
the scriptures; and that he was buried, and that he
rose again the third day according to the scriptures"
(vv. 3,4). That is good news! That is what Christ has
done for us. We may accept it and receive it now by
faith, by faith alone.

Just as the throne of Ahasuerus protected the Jews
when Esther and Mordecai interceded, the very throne
of God protects us today. The apostle says, "Who shall
lay any thing to the charge of God's elect? It is God
that justifieth. Who is he that condemneth? It is Christ
that died, yea rather, that is risen again, who is even at
the right hand of God, who also maketh intercession
for us" (Rom. 8:33,34). Notice how He justifies: (1)
Christ died; (2) He is risen again; (3) He is even at the
right hand of God; (4) He also makes intercession for
us. These are the reasons no one can condemn a believer. How wonderful this is! Today there is a *Man* in
the realms of glory—He knows exactly how you feel,
and He knows exactly how I feel. And in that position
He is interceding for us. How wonderful to know that

we have Someone there for us. Things have changed for us sinners.

> Seeing then that we have a great high priest, that is passed into the heavens, Jesus the Son of God, let us hold fast our profession. For we have not an high priest which cannot be touched with the feeling of our infirmities; but was in all points tempted like as we are, yet without sin. Let us therefore come boldly unto the throne of grace, that we may obtain mercy, and find grace to help in time of need (Heb. 4:14–16).

Go back with me now to some little unknown village in one of the 127 provinces of the Persian empire. Possibly way out in the hinterland there was a community in which there were a few Jews. When they saw the decree, they looked at it and said, "We don't believe it," and paid no attention to the second decree of the king at all. I'm of the opinion that all of them perished. All they needed to do was to believe the king and act upon that belief in faith, and God would have delivered them.

Today God saves all sinners who will *act* upon the marvelous new decree of grace that He has sent out into the world: "Believe on the Lord Jesus Christ, and thou shalt be saved . . ." (Acts 16:31).

Let's look again at the theme of the Book of Esther: the providence of God. Although God's people in the days of Queen Esther had rejected Him, and He had withdrawn His name from them, they were not out of the reach of His providence. God preserved His people, and by His providence He still was gracious to them.

If you are a child of God, do not be led by God's

providence. Do not be like the horse that must be led forcibly by a bridle. Being led by His providence is the method He uses with those who rebel at being led. If you are His child, He wants to lead you directly. He says, "I will instruct thee and teach thee in the way which thou shalt go: I will guide thee with mine eye" (Ps. 32:8). This requires a blessed nearness to God if we are to have the guidance of His eye. God wants to direct us and touch our lives in an intimate way. But how many Christians are sensitive to the leading of the Holy Spirit in this day? God will not bring much pressure to bear, but when He makes just a little suggestion to you at the crossroads of life, are you too far from Him to know that He is indicating a certain pathway? You and I as believers should not be guided by the providence of God; we ought to be guided directly by the Spirit of God.

Yet even if we slip out from under God's *direct* dealings, we have not slipped out from under His *providential* dealings. God ever stands in the shadows, keeping watch over His own.